Formerly
New Directions for
Mental Health Services

Gil G. Noam
Editor-in-Chief

W9-BMV-517

NEW DIRECTIONS FOR YOUTH DEVELOPMENT

Theory
Practice
Research

fall | 2002

Pathways to Positive Development Among Diverse Youth

Richard M. Lerner
Carl S. Taylor
Alexander von Eye

issue
editors

JOSSEY-BASS
A Wiley Imprint
www.josseybass.com

Pathways to Positive Development Among Diverse Youth
Richard M. Lerner, Carl S. Taylor, Alexander von Eye (eds.)
New Directions for Youth Development, No. 95, Fall 2002
Gil G. Noam, Editor-in-Chief

Microfilm copies of issues and articles are available in 16mm and 35mm, as well as microfiche in 105mm, through University Microfilms Inc., 300 North Zeeb Road, Ann Arbor, Michigan 48106-1346.

ISSN 1533-8916 (print)   ISSN 1537-5781 (online)   ISBN 0-7879-6338-0 (print)

New Directions for Youth Development is part of The Jossey-Bass Psychology Series and is published quarterly by Wiley Subscription Services, Inc., A Wiley Company, at Jossey-Bass, 989 Market Street, San Francisco, California 94103-1741. Periodicals postage paid at San Francisco, California, and at additional mailing offices. Postmaster: Send address changes to New Directions for Youth Development, Jossey-Bass, 989 Market Street, San Francisco, California 94103-1741.

Subscriptions cost $75.00 for individuals and $149.00 for institutions, agencies, and libraries. Prices subject to change. Refer to the order form at the back of this issue.

Editorial correspondence should be sent to the Editor-in-Chief, Dr. Gil G. Noam, Harvard Graduate School of Education, Larsen Hall 601, Appian Way, Cambridge, MA 02138 or McLean Hospital, 115 Mill Street, Belmont, MA 02478.

Cover photograph by Getty Images.

Jossey-Bass Web address: www.josseybass.com

Contents

1. Positive youth development: Thriving as the basis of personhood
   and civil society   *11*
   Richard M. Lerner, Cornelia Brentano, Elizabeth M. Dowling,
   Pamela M. Anderson
   Theoretical issues pertinent to a developmental systems understanding of
   positive youth development, and to the role of thriving processes and civic
   engagement in such development, are discussed.

2. Stability of attributes of positive functioning and of developmental assets among African American adolescent male gang and
   community-based organization members   *35*
   Carl S. Taylor, Richard M. Lerner, Alexander von Eye,
   Aida Bilalbegovic Balsano, Elizabeth M. Dowling,
   Pamela M. Anderson, Deborah L. Bobek, Dragana Bjelobrk
   Longitudinal analysis of positive functioning and of individual and ecological developmental assets among African American male youth involved in
   gangs or in community-based organizations provides evidence for the
   potential of positive development among both adolescent groups.

3. Individual and ecological assets and positive developmental trajec-
   tories among gang and community-based organization youth   *57*
   Carl S. Taylor, Richard M. Lerner, Alexander von Eye,
   Aida Bilalbegovic Balsano, Elizabeth M. Dowling,
   Pamela M. Anderson, Deborah L. Bobek, Dragana Bjelobrk
   Across a one-year longitudinal assessment, both individual and ecological
   assets are linked to positive developmental trajectories among African
   American male youth involved in gangs and in community-based organiza-
   tions serving youth.

4. Identity processes and the positive development of African
   Americans: An explanatory framework   *73*
   Dena Phillips Swanson, Margaret Beale Spencer, Tabitha
   Dell'Angelo, Vinay Harpalani, Tirzah R. Spencer

Spencer's phenomenological variant of ecological systems theory frames an understanding of positive youth development and of the contextual and individual factors promoting it among African American adolescents.

Issue Editors' Notes

ADAPTIVE REGULATION of behavior across the life span has been the focus of developmental research aimed at understanding how adolescents, amid the internal and contextual changes prototypic of this period of life, maintain positive, healthy trajectories. Current developmental systems theoretical models of adolescent development stress that individual differences in the positive or negative outcomes of adolescent regulatory behavior—of the processes that enable their resiliency—are produced by their history of person-context relations. These relations involve individual and contextual variables, seen as "fused" within a dynamic developmental system.

Recently, such models have been devised to understand the characteristics of change across life of racially, ethnically, and culturally diverse youth—specifically, the resiliency, or "adaptive mode," used by these adolescents and their family and community contexts to promote positive development. This emphasis on positive youth development constitutes a significant innovation in research, particularly within the adolescent period where young people are engaging in negative, unhealthy behaviors at a historically unprecedented level. The probability of engagement in adolescent problem behavior (for example, delinquency, violence, substance use, unsafe sex) is associated with poverty, and race is the single best predictor of poverty and its behavioral sequelae.

Yet amid such trends there are also numerous success stories of positive developmental outcomes among poor youth of color. For instance, there are many instances of positive, healthy development of African American male adolescents—arguably the group with the highest probability of experiencing the problematic behaviors associated with race and poverty in America. There is evidence that

NEW DIRECTIONS FOR YOUTH DEVELOPMENT, NO. 95, FALL 2002 © WILEY PERIODICALS, INC.

the bases of positive development of these youth—of their ability to "overcome the odds" against their positive development—lie in combinations of individual and ecological characteristics.

Given these data about the linkages among individual and ecological variables and positive development, this monograph discusses the theoretical, research, policy, and program dimensions of taking a strength-based, positive development approach to diverse youth. Theoretical ideas about the nature of positive youth development, and about the related concepts of thriving and well-being, are presented. In addition, there is discussion of current and needed policy strategies and of best practice in youth-serving programs and community-based efforts to marshal the developmental assets of individuals and communities to enhance thriving among young people. These issues of theory and application are illustrated by using data derived from several research centers seeking to better understand and enhance the lives of diverse youth.

First, findings are presented from an ongoing longitudinal study—termed "Overcoming the Odds" (OTO)—of the individual and ecological assets present among African American adolescent males living in poor, inner-city neighborhoods and involved either in a gang or a community-based, youth-serving organization. The goal of OTO is to identify the individual and contextual conditions that may protect African American male youth from actualizing risk (meaning, that may allow them to overcome the odds) and that in turn may promote positive (healthy, successful) development.

Data from OTO bear on key developmental systems theoretical ideas about the person-context relational character of human development and about the need for mutually beneficial alignment (that is, fostering resiliency, or promoting positive regulations) between individuals and institutions. Specifically, OTO is predicated on two instances of developmental systems models consistent with this perspective about the bases of positive youth development. The first is Margaret Beale Spencer's conception of ascertaining the "adaptive modes" used by children and youths of color to adjust to and prosper in their contexts; more generally OTO is predicated on her integrative approach to understanding, through her "phenomenological variant of ecological systems theory" (or PVEST) model, the role of multiple levels of the context on ethnic identity. The second is the work of Peter L. Benson and his colleagues at Search Institute on identifying individual and ecological developmental assets and on promoting positive development—and indeed, thriving—through integrating developmental assets across the adolescent years within the diverse communities of America. As such, reports from Spencer and her colleagues and from Benson are included in this issue.

The scholarship about positive youth development in the OTO project and in the work of Spencer and Benson is consistent as well with applied developmental research efforts to understand and deploy in systemic interventions the interrelated developmental and contextual bases of resilience among diverse young people. A leading center for such scholarship is led by Suniya S. Luthar, whose efforts have involved use of a person-context transactional model of developmental psychopathology to study risk and positive development among poor, inner-city youth and affluent adolescents living in wealthy suburban settings. She describes the nature and results of her program of work in this volume.

Finally, all research centers represented in this volume stress, within their respective ecological or developmental systems perspectives, the need to engage collaboratively all individuals and institutions within the community in the service of youth. The William T. Grant Foundation has championed a vision of such communitywide, asset-integrating efforts to support making progress in American society in fostering healthy developmental pathways for youth. Robert C. Granger, executive vice president of the foundation, describes a new conceptual model for understanding the range of interventions that may be used to create intentional change in the developmental system to promote positive youth development. He explains that these interventions encompass strategies seeking to enhance among people, organizations, communities, or systems either the will to institute efforts for such change or the capacity for furthering such change. The perspective and efforts of this foundation offer a capstone vision for the volume in regard to future directions for integrated research and practice activities seeking to enhance the life chances of all youth and to increase the probability of their leading lives marked by psychosocial and physical health and thriving.

In sum, this issue discusses how theory, research, and applications may fit our needs to create effective, appropriately scaled, and sustainable pathways for developing healthy and productive young people. All contributions to the volume share the vision that successful efforts to promote positive youth development rest on moving beyond prevention strategies, to research and practice intended to promote thriving and development through preparing youths to become fully engaged, active citizens. In such work, all sectors of society—and, most centrally, young people and their families—must be active, productive, and collaborative partners.

Richard M. Lerner
Carl S. Taylor
Alexander von Eye
Issue Editors

Executive Summary

1. Positive youth development: Thriving as the basis of personhood and civil society

Richard M. Lerner, Cornelia Brentano, Elizabeth M. Dowling, Pamela M. Anderson

This chapter describes the foundations for thriving during adolescence. According to developmental systems theories, thriving is conceptualized as adaptive regulation that involves mutually beneficial and sustaining exchange between individuals and contexts (such as the family, peer group, or community). This process includes both universal structural components and culturally specific functional components. Thriving youth become productive adults through progressive enhancement of behaviors that are valued in their specific society and that reflect the structural value of contributing to civil society. An integrated moral and civic identity and a commitment to society beyond one's own existence enable youth to be agents of their own healthy development and of positive change in people and society.

2. Stability of attributes of positive functioning and of developmental assets among African American adolescent male gang and community-based organization members

Carl S. Taylor, Richard M. Lerner, Alexander von Eye, Aida Bilalbegovic Balsano, Elizabeth M. Dowling, Pamela M. Anderson, Deborah L. Bobek, Dragana Bjelobrk

NEW DIRECTIONS FOR YOUTH DEVELOPMENT, NO. 95, FALL 2002 © WILEY PERIODICALS, INC.

Stability was assessed over the course of one year in scores for attributes of positive functioning and for individual and ecological developmental assets—those internal and external qualities that help youth thrive. Data were derived from individual interviews conducted in 1999 and 2000 with forty-five African American adolescent male members of inner-city Detroit gangs and fifty African American adolescent youths living in the same communities but involved in community-based organizations (CBOs) aimed at promoting positive youth development. Analyses indicated that both groups showed stability for attribute and developmental asset scores and that these scores were more often significantly interrelated over time among the gang members than among the CBO youth. Idiographic analyses of intraindividual fluctuation in changes across time and in the changes indicative of growth in positive functioning offered evidence that among gang youth, even more so than among the CBO youth, change was linked to developmental assets. These analyses suggested that when gang youth are linked in their ecology to developmental assets, the potential exists for their "overcoming the odds." The import of the findings for programs and policies—that all youth possess potential for positive development—is discussed.

---

3. Individual and ecological assets and positive developmental trajectories among gang and community-based organization youth

Carl S. Taylor, Richard M. Lerner, Alexander von Eye, Aida Bilalbegovic Balsano, Elizabeth M. Dowling, Pamela M. Anderson, Deborah L. Bobek, Dragana Bjelobrk

As in the preceding chapter, data were derived from individual interviews conducted in 1999 and 2000 with forty-five African American adolescent male members of inner-city Detroit gangs and fifty African American adolescent males living in the same communities but involved in community-based organizations (CBOs) aimed at promoting positive youth development. Interviews assessed the presence of attributes of positive functioning (for example, in regard to family, peers, and identity) and developmental assets related to individual functioning (such as positive values) and ecological supports (for instance, empowerment). For both groups, developmental assets were related to positive functioning. Of particular theoretical significance, developmental assets at both times of testing were related to positive functioning among gang youth. We discuss the import of the findings for programs and policies that all youth possess a stable potential for positive development.

4. Identity processes and the positive development of African Americans: An explanatory framework

Dena Phillips Swanson, Margaret Beale Spencer, Tabitha Dell'Angelo, Vinay Harpalani, Tirzah R. Spencer

How do we understand the interactive and complex characteristics of adolescents' identity development, and support positive, resilient outcomes among youth? In this chapter, the phenomenological variant of ecological systems theory (PVEST) is used to discuss the links between positive development among African American youth and identity and self-appraisal processes and, as well, later-life outcomes. The authors examine the impact on African American adolescents of such contextual factors as school, religious institutions, social stereotypes, community, and culture on racial and gender identity, and on related constructs such as body image. They discuss the significance of identity-related coping strategies in response to life events as a means to develop positively in the face of contextual challenges. The chapter emphasizes the importance for youth of engaging in productive activity as a buffer against negative contextual experiences and to promote well-being, irrespective of race—especially the significance of involvement in a religious institution and of spirituality in the lives of young people.

5. Adolescent risk: The costs of affluence

Suniya S. Luthar, Shawn J. Latendresse

The authors discuss the impact of affluence on the presence of risk behaviors among adolescents through use of a developmental psychopathology model that emphasizes the significance of transactions among contexts (family, peers, school, culture) and the coherence of development across the life span. The chapter presents evidence that problems of youth development, and the contextual conditions related to them, exist comparably among poor, inner-city youth and wealthier adolescents. For instance, in comparing inner-city high school youth and suburban youth, both groups experienced emotional distress and substance abuse; interestingly, the affluent group had higher scores for these problems than did the inner-city one. Moreover, affluent middle school youth were similar to their affluent high school counterparts. Achievement pressure and disconnection from parents may be sources of maladjustment among these affluent adolescents. The authors highlight the comparability between these findings and recent media reports about affluent youth.

6. Adolescent development in social and community context: A program of research

Peter L. Benson

In the last decade, Search Institute in Minneapolis has designed and launched research initiatives intended to understand the combination of community and social changes needed to increase access to and utilization of a series of "developmental nutrients," or assets. Drawing on ideas from several disciplines—including community development, developmental psychology, sociology, and anthropology—and integrating both quantitative and qualitative studies of adolescent development in American communities, this chapter explores the linkages among developmental ecologies, adolescent development, risk behavior, and thriving. The article synthesizes this body of research and offers recommendations for crafting a line of research dedicated to exploring pathways to developmental success.

7. Creating the conditions linked to positive youth development

Robert C. Granger

There is growing agreement about several conditions needed to create intentional change in the developmental system. This chapter proposes a framework for conceptualizing interventions that promote positive youth development. The framework is based on improving the support and opportunities for change in the conditions linked to positive youth development. These interventions involve strategies meant to enhance either the will or the capacity to change among individuals, organizations, systems, and communities. The author examines the implications of this framework for future research and practice.

Positive youth development is conceptualized within a developmental systems theoretical model. The role of thriving processes and civic engagement in positive youth development is discussed.

1

Positive youth development: Thriving as the basis of personhood and civil society

Richard M. Lerner, Cornelia Brentano,
Elizabeth M. Dowling, Pamela M. Anderson

IN THESE EARLIEST YEARS of the twenty-first century, a new vision and vocabulary for discussing America's young people has emerged. Propelled by the increasingly collaborative contributions of scholars,[1] practitioners,[2] and policy makers,[3] youth are viewed as resources to be developed. The vocabulary emerging to discuss the strengths present within all young people involves such concepts as developmental assets,[4] positive youth development,[5] moral development,[6] civic engagement,[7] well-being,[8] and thriving.[9] All these concepts are predicated on the ideas that *every* young person has the potential for successful, healthy development and that *all* youth possess the capacity for positive development.

Note: The writing of this article was supported in part by grants from the W. T. Grant Foundation and the National 4-H Council. Further information about this research can be obtained from Richard M. Lerner, Eliot-Pearson Department of Child Development, 105 College Ave., Tufts University, Medford, MA 02155.

NEW DIRECTIONS FOR YOUTH DEVELOPMENT, NO. 95, FALL 2002 © WILEY PERIODICALS, INC.

The vision for and vocabulary about youth have evolved over the course of a scientifically arduous path.[10] Complicating any new conceptualization of the character of youth as a resource for positive development of self, family, and community was an antithetical theoretical approach to the nature and development of young people. The alternative perspective was characterized by a deficit view.[11] Beginning at least in G. Stanley Hall's foundational, two-volume work about adolescence,[12] which emphasized that this period of life was inevitably characterized by "storm and stress," during much of the past century many scholars followed a model that treated youth as "problems to be managed."[13] These scholars discussed young people with a vocabulary that emphasized weakness and inadequacy, and with a perspective believing that problems of mental and behavioral functioning were inevitable unless preventive action was instituted at developmentally propitious times.

This deficit view was coupled with the idea that the problems of youth were atypical at best, and at worst psychopathological deviation from normal developmental processes. Therefore, understanding such deviation was not seen as being of direct relevance to scholarship aimed at discovering the principles of basic developmental processes. Accordingly, the characteristics of youth were regarded as issues of "only" applied concern—and thus of secondary scientific interest. Not only did this model separate basic science from application but it also disembedded the adolescent from the study of normal or healthy development. In short, the deficit view of youth as problems to be managed split the study of young people from the study of health and positive development.[14]

Other types of split were associated with this deficit model of youth development. The conception of developmental process typically associated with this model often involved a causal split between individual and context, between organism and environment, or—most generally—between nature and nurture.[15] Theories based on this model emphasized either a predetermined organismic basis of development—as in attachment theory,[16] ethological theory,[17] behavioral genetics,[18] psychoanalytic theory,[19] neopsychoanalytic theory,[20] or environmentally reductionistic and mechanistic behavioral theory.[21] For instance, within such views the "pathology" of young people was reduced to bad genes, insensitive parenting, socialization failure, or other "single" causes.

Other theories stressed more of an interaction between organismic and environmental sources of development.[22] Nevertheless, there remained a presupposition that there were two distinct sources of development—a split between organism and environment. As such, it was the role of theory to explain the contributions of these two separate domains of reality to human development.[23]

In short, scholars studying human development in general and youth development in particular used a theoretical model incapable of useful deployment in understanding either the relational nature of development[24] or the synthesis between basic and applied science. Such a split conception was also involved in separating the study of young people from appraisal of normative, healthy, or positive development. However, the integration of person and context, of basic and applied scholarship, and of young people with the potential for positive development was legitimated by the relational models of development that emerged by the end of the twentieth century to define the cutting edge of developmental scholarship.[25]

Developmental systems, relative plasticity, and regulation of person-context relations

The forefront of contemporary developmental theory and research is associated with ideas stressing that systemic (bidirectional, fused) *relations* between individuals and contexts constitute the basis of human behavior and developmental change.[26] The stress in contemporary developmental theories is on accounting for how the integrated developmental system functions. Within the context of such a theory, changes across the life span are seen as propelled by the dynamic relations between the individual and the multiple levels of the ecology of human development (family, peer group, school, community, culture), all changing interdependently across time (history).[27]

Temporal embeddedness means there always exists, across the life span, the potential for change in person-context relations. There are two important concepts associated with this optimistic view of the potential to enhance human life. Developmental regulation is, as has been implied, one of these concepts. Developmental systems ideas about this regulation derive from the other important concept, that of relative plasticity. Relative plasticity and developmental regulation frame a conceptualization of a life-span developmental process that may be labeled as "thriving." Because thriving integrates attributes of the person and the social context, adaptive developmental regulation necessarily enhances development of self and of society.

By explaining the implications of relative plasticity and developmental regulation for the thriving process, we argue, first, that bidirectional person-context relations create in individual development a sense of the transcendent significance of contributing integratively to self and society. Second, we explain how these concepts frame understanding of the importance for healthy human development of a socially just, democratic, civil society. Third, these ideas enable understanding of why the specific features of person-context relations constitute a life-span developmental process (thriving), and why this process necessarily involves moral development, civic engagement, and spiritual development among youth.

Implications of plasticity for positive youth development

Although the relationship of individual ontogeny to history means that change is a necessary feature of human life, change in person-context relations is of course not limitless. Interlevel relations within the system both facilitate and constrain the opportunity for change; it is constrained by past developments and by contemporary contextual conditions. As a consequence, contemporary developmental systems theories stress that *relative plasticity*—the potential for systematic change in structure or function—exists throughout life, although the magnitude of this plasticity may vary across ontogeny.[28]

The presence of relative plasticity legitimates an optimistic and proactive search for characteristics of individuals and their ecologies that, together, can be arrayed to promote positive developmental change.[29] Accordingly, the developmental systems' stress on relative plasticity is a foundation for an applied developmental science aimed at enhancing human development through strengthening the linkages between developing individuals and their changing family and community settings. From this applied developmental science perspective, healthy development involves positive change in the relation between a developing person—who is committed and able to contribute positively to self, family, and community—and a community supporting the development of such a citizen.

As defined here, a young person may be said to be *thriving* if he or she is involved over time in such healthy, positive relations with his or her community, and on the path to what Csikszentmihalyi and Rathunde[30] describe as "idealized personhood" (an adult status marked by making culturally valued contributions to self, others, and institutions). Thus the components of the individual-psychological and social-relational features of person-context relations that change over time to constitute such development make up the thriving process. Figure 1.1 illustrates the components of the person-context relations that (we argue later) structure the thriving process among youth.

Applied developmental science and the thriving process

Applied developmental science efforts that promote thriving may involve enhancing a person's orientation to contribute to healthy family life and democratic community institutions while, at the same time, improving oneself in a manner that enables one's individual actions to be successful. That orientation can be seen in promotion of a sense of the importance of levels of being beyond the self—that is, a sense of spirituality,[31] and of the importance of undertaking a role to contribute to social well-being (a moral identity, a sense of civic duty).[32] Simultaneously, such applied developmental science work may involve furthering the institutions and systems within a community to facilitate healthy development.[33]

Figure 1.1. A developmental contextual view of the thriving process

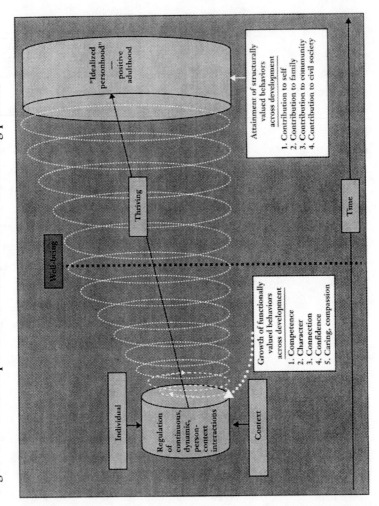

Examples of such efforts are giving young people the opportunity to contribute to and take a leadership position in community efforts to improve social life and social justice and, over time, to develop their commitment to and skill at community building.[34]

The basis for change in person-context relations, and for both plasticity and constraint in development, lies in the relations that exist among the multiple levels of organization constituting the substance of human life.[35] Accordingly, applied developmental science efforts aimed at furthering the thriving process, and at fostering in young people a spiritual sense and a moral commitment to make a healthy, integrated contribution to self, family, community, and civil society, may involve work focused on multiple levels of organization within the developmental system. These levels range from the inner biological, through the individual-psychological and the proximal social-relational (involving dyads, peer groups, and nuclear families), to the sociocultural (including key macro institutions such as educational, public policy, governmental, and economic systems) and the natural and designed physical ecologies of human development.[36]

Developmental regulation and the thriving process

Within developmental systems theories, changing relations are the basic unit of analysis. [37] As such, regulation of these relations across development must be a central concern in efforts directed to capitalize positively on the relative plasticity of the human developmental system to enhance healthy behavior and development. As emphasized throughout this chapter, such developmental regulation involves mutually beneficial and sustaining exchanges between individuals and contexts. At the level of individual functioning, successful (adaptive, health-promoting) regulations involve changing the self to support the context and altering the context to support the self; such efforts require the individual to remain committed to contributing to the context and to possess, or strive to develop, the skills for making such a contribution.

Accordingly, applied developmental efforts aimed at creating and sustaining effective (healthy) person-context regulations may be directed, on the one hand, toward enhancing the person's self-definition or moral sense in regard to embracing the significance of enhancing social justice and democracy and, on the other hand, toward improving the systems present within the social context to enable individual freedom and facilitate equity and opportunity for all individuals. When these respective contributions are synthesized over time in a manner that involves increased thriving of individuals, there is a growth in the institutions of civil society, in the "space" between people and government.[38] A system of positive human development is therefore present.

In short, a social system that celebrates individuality and individual initiative will be one that individuals seek to serve and sustain. Such a relation is the essence of the mutual person-context benefits defining adaptive developmental regulation. This regulation has fundamental biological significance.

Evolutionary bases of person-context developmental regulation

The story of human evolution is one of neoteny (that is, a slowed rate of development relative to ancestral species) and of social interdependence between individuals and groups.[39] The protohominid ancestors of humans were initially small (in overall size and in brain matter), tree-dwelling, herbivorous creatures that, except for mating during the female's estrus cycle, lived largely solitary lives.[40] However, as the lush African rain forest changed to savannah, several interrelated changes were involved in a succession of evolutionary events that led from these protohominids to humans.

Five to seven million years ago, humans emerged on the African savannah as large-brained creatures with a protracted period of postnatal development within which to develop into maturity. This long period of childhood enabled the young to organize their brains in an environment richer and more complex than that in utero and afforded the young the opportunity to learn about the social world within which they were embedded.[41] Having no sharp teeth and claws, humans were relatively defenseless. Social organization was needed for individual survival—for instance, to organize a hunting party and to protect against predators.[42]

Large-brained humans were able to devise weapons to improve hunting and protection, as well as tools for scavenging and cooking and early agricultural innovations. In addition, role divisions emerged. The more muscular, male members of the group undertook hunting duties. In turn, their female counterparts—in relation to the emergence of menstrual cycles—created with the males the biosocial innovation of pair bonding. As a consequence, the females undertook the job of caring for newborn, immature, and slowly developing offspring.[43]

From the beginning of their existence, then, humans have been linked to a social world for their survival. The social world—the people and institutions of society—needed individuals who learned to be committed to protecting, contributing to, and perpetuating the group. The individual needed the group—society—for a supportive context ensuring both survival and the opportunity to develop the physical, mental, and behavioral characteristics requisite for making a mature contribution to self and society. [44]

Individual and societal interests and needs have been inextricably integrated across the course of human evolution (phylogeny); the story of healthy human development from birth to maturity (ontogeny) is one of understanding regulation over the life span of individual-context relations, of ascertaining how the relation between an individual's actions on the context and the context's actions on the individual occurs or may be fostered in a way that promotes personhood marked by health and societal maintenance, perpetuation, and enhancement. [45]

Structural and functional components of developmental regulation

Healthy and successful development of young people may be understood within the context of human evolution and of how adaptive regulation of person-context relations constitutes the basic process of ontogenetic change within the developmental system. This process has been conceptualized here as thriving. From the perspective of the integrated levels of organization composing this developmental system, there are universal, structural, and cultural or society-specific functional components of a developmental linkage between the person and context that enables thriving to occur.

The universal components of the developmental process constituting thriving involve the structure of the regulatory connection between person and context. From a developmental systems perspective, one informed by the neotenous character of human evolution, the key unit of analysis in studying human development is the integrated relation between the individual level of organization and the multilevel ecology of human development. This ecology is composed of other people (peer groups, families) and the institutions of society and culture that are constituted both physically (schools, religious institutions) and conceptually or ideologically (the values that exist in a society in regard to the desired features of human functioning).

Within the developmental system, a relation that subserves maintenance and perpetuation of the system is one wherein the individual acts to support the institutions of society and, simultaneously, wherein these institutions support the healthy and productive functioning and development of the individual.[46] In such a relation, the actions of the individual on the context and the actions of the context on the individual are fused in producing healthy outcomes for the individual and the institutions.[47]

As such, the key feature of the thriving process is regulation of person-context relations eventuating in such multilevel outcomes.[48] In fact, a critical structural value of all societies—indeed a universal structural value of all societies—is that an individual's regulation of person-context relations makes positive contributions to self, family, community, and society.[49] In short, then, in all societies healthy and valued personhood is seen as a period, or "stage," wherein such generative regulation exists.[50]

Of course, there is variation among societies as to what a person must do to manifest such structural values of productive and healthy personhood. That is, how a person must function to manifest structurally valued regulation varies from one social/cultural setting to another and with historical (and ecological) conditions.[51] Functional values show social, cultural, and temporal variation. For example, in the United States, regulations that support individual freedom, equity, and democracy are highly valued. It may be that in other societies regulations supporting interindividually invariant belief in and/or obedience to religious dictums is of superordinate value.

In every case, however, the society shows variation within a given historical moment as to which behaviors are judged to be valuable in (consistent with) supporting the universal structural value of maintaining or perpetuating person-context regulations subserving mutually beneficial individual and institutional relations.[52] As a consequence, the markers or indices of what an individual must manifest as he or she develops from infancy to adult personhood may vary with place and time.[53] Accordingly, there may be variation across societies and points in time within the same society in defining person-context relations that foster positive youth development—and thus variation in the specific behaviors that move a young person along a life path wherein he or she possesses the functional values of society and attains structurally valued personhood. Simply, there may be historical and cultural variation in the specific, functionally valued components of the thriving process.

Thriving as a marker of healthy and successful developmental regulations

Whatever the specific behaviors involved in thriving at a given time or in a particular place, within developmental systems theories thriving invariantly involves a young person manifesting a systematic enhancement across his or her ontogeny behaviors that function to enhance developmental regulation. This invariance exists because of the linkage between such growth and attainment in adulthood of structurally valued behaviors—that is, behaviors that maintain, perpetuate, and enhance self and context. As such, thriving is a developmental concept that denotes a healthy change process linking a youth with an adulthood status enabling society to be populated by healthy individuals oriented to integratively serve self and civil society.

In essence, then, adaptive developmental regulation results in the emergence among young people of an orientation to transcend self-interest and place value on, and commit to, action supportive of a social system promoting equity, democracy, social justice, and personal freedom. This sort of system is one that enables the individual and individual initiative to prosper. As such, it is this relation—between an individual engaged in support of a democratic system and a democratic system that supports the individual—that is the essence of the mutual, person-context benefits defining healthy developmental regulation.

Developing such integrated moral and civic identity in youth requires community systems and cultural institutions that integrate individual and ecological developmental assets.[54] and, through such synthesis, promote civil society. This society is characterized by a social ecological space between individuals and government that creates, brings to scale, and sustains institutions effective in ensuring social justice and equity for all people.[55] The presence of a civil society reflects the ideal relation between the development of the individual and a democratic social system.

Within the frame of this model, the thriving process comprises dynamic (bidirectional, reciprocal) person-context relations that involve institutional support of behaviors that are valued by society because they serve the function of enabling young people to develop an internalized orientation (moral commitment, civically engaged self definition, and the spiritual sense of the meaningfulness of being part of an existence that transcends the self in time and place). Such development enables youth to become adults who, ideally, contribute to self and context in a way that maintains and perpetuates the social order *and* advances social justice and civil society.

Well-being is a term that can be used to denote within-time person-context exchanges that are associated with healthy functioning.[56] However, as seen from the perspective of developmental systems theory, thriving is a developmental process embracing changes in youth-context relations that culminate in attainment of the idealized personhood[57] noted earlier—that is, enactment in adulthood of behaviors that contribute positively to the healthy structure of society and, in so doing, support and further self, family, community, and civil society.

Adaptive developmental regulation creates in young people behaviors valuable for positive person-context functioning, behaviors such as the "five C's" of positive youth development: competence, confidence, character, social connection, and caring (or compassion).[58] As a result of such positive youth development, young people develop an orientation to contribute to their community. Developing such functionally valued behaviors in young people—as well as developing understanding of and commitment to entities that transcend self and self-interest—results in the emergence in youth of an orientation to contribute to their community (contribution being a "sixth C" of positive youth development [59]).

A commitment to contributing rests on defining behavior in support of mutually beneficial person-context exchanges as being morally necessary. Individuals' moral duty to contribute exists because, as citizens receiving benefits from a social system supporting their individual functioning, it is necessary to be actively engaged in (at the least maintaining and ideally enhancing) that social system. [60]

Thriving and spiritual development

The sense of transcendence of self and of zero-sum-game self-interest that accrues as integrated moral and civic self-definitions (identities) develop may be interpreted as a growing spiritual sense.[61] Erikson[62] discussed the emotional "virtues" coupled with successful resolution of each of the eight psychosocial crises he postulated in his theory of ego development. He specified that fidelity, defined as unflagging commitment to abstract ideas beyond the self (for example, an ideology), was the virtue associated with adaptive resolution of the identity crisis of adolescence, and thus with attainment of a socially prescribed, positive role.[63] Commitment to a role was regarded by Erikson[64] as a means for the behaviors of youth to serve the maintenance and perpetuation of society; fidelity to the ideology coupled with the role meant that the young person would gain emotional satisfaction—which, to Erikson,[65] meant enhanced self-esteem—through contributing to society by enacting role behaviors.[66]

One need not focus only on crisis resolution to suggest that behaviors attained during adolescence in the service of identity development may be coupled with an ideological "virtue," that is, with a sensibility about the meaningfulness of abstract ideas that transcend the self.[67] From a perspective that focuses on adaptive developmental regulation within the developmental system, it is possible to suggest that spirituality is the transcendent virtue coupled with the behaviors (roles) predicated on the emergence of an integrated moral and civic identity.

There is evidence of a marked increase in the adolescent years in spirituality, although not in commitment to an organized religious institution.[68] These data suggest that individual identity development, reflecting a moral and civic engagement or commitment to society, is fused with spiritual development in adolescence.[69]

As such, a youth whose exchange with his or her context (whose developmental regulation) is marked by functionally valued behavior should develop an integrated moral and civic identity and a transcendent, or spiritual, sensibility.[70] Such development puts the young person on a path to becoming an adult citizen making generative contributions to self, family, community, and civil society. A youth producing these valued behaviors is manifesting what we have specified as the essence of the thriving process.

Indexing the thriving process among youth

At any point in time, a young person may show a unitemporal pattern of covariation among indices of these valued behaviors. As implied earlier, in such a case the young person may be said to be in a state of well-being. For example, cross-sectionally, well-being that is indexed by variables pertinent to the five C's, by the sixth C (contribution), or by some integration of these concepts, should co-vary with indices of successful person-context regulation (as represented by measures of selection, optimization, and compensation, or SOC).[71]

Because thriving is a process concept, longitudinal analysis is needed to adequately appraise whether there is evidence that patterns of covariation exist over time in a manner reflecting the growth of person-context relations promoting individual health and civil society. From a developmental systems perspective, a youth who is thriving is engaged in person-context regulatory processes that eventuate in healthy and productive adult personhood. [72]

Thriving may be indexed, therefore, by developmental changes indicative of integrated, positive change in the mental and behavioral life of a young person. Mentally, there should be evidence of a growing moral and civic identity and of the virtue of spirituality that, with such identity development, accompanies commitment to a concern with existence that transcends the self. Behaviorally, thriving may be indexed by better (healthier, more positive) performance in regard to the functional values of society and by enhanced regulatory action. Such action constitutes performance consistent with structural values—in other words, with person-context interactions that link the person positively to the institutions of civil society.

If thriving is developing in this manner, then across the developmental system there should be changes in the contextual resources for such development, especially because thriving youth are civically engaged youth who are morally committed to enhancing these resources. Thriving young people epitomize the idea, found in the developmental contextual version of developmental systems theory,[73] that individuals are producers of their own development.

Accordingly, within a community embracing thriving, young people's institutional resources and actions promoting the thriving process should be evident and changing positively across time. Such contextual conditions are reflected by the individual and ecological developmental assets identified by Search Institute as the key basis for thriving among youth.[74] As well, these thriving-supportive conditions may be manifested by the youth-community integration summarized by Damon[75] in his concept of the youth charter. Whatever the constitution of these developmental assets, because of the growing moral and civic identity of a thriving youth, a young person who is thriving becomes a person contributing effectively to maintaining and perpetuating these same community assets.

Thus, within a developmental systems model of the person-context regulatory processes involved in healthy youth development, and in positive and productive adult personhood, young people and their communities are involved in a bidirectional relationship wherein community assets are both a product and a producer of the actions of engaged young people. These young people are thriving in that they are changing in a direction indicative of enhanced performance of behavior (functions) valued in their specific society (competence, confidence, connection, and so forth) and are, as a consequence, embedded in person-context regulations (for example, as indexed by SOC) that reflect the structural value of contributing to civil society. Thriving youth become generative adults.[76] Such adults productively build the assets of their community and manifest the moral orientation, spirituality, and behavioral commitment to ensure for themselves, their families, and their broader social world the quality, scale, and sustainability of the institutions of social justice and civil society.

As noted earlier, Figure 1 illustrates the pattern of person-context relations envisioned within the structural model of the youth thriving process that we have described. The structural model presented in this figure presents a potential frame for discussing the design and psychometric issues needed to devise a change-sensitive measure of thriving and to employ it in longitudinal research documenting the role of thriving in positive youth development. Such research can chart the nature and bases of the emergence of an individual making a significant contribution to the family and to moral and civil society.

Conclusion

Developmentally emergent and contextually mediated successful regulation of positive person-context relations ensures that individuals have the nurturance and support needed for healthy development. Simultaneously, such regulation produces, for society, people having the mental and behavioral capacities—the inner and outer lives—requisite to maintain, perpetuate, and enhance socially just, equitable, and democratic social institutions.[77]

To sustain the individual and societal benefits of these person-context relations, socialization must promote (1) a moral orientation among youth that good is created through contributing to positive person-context relations; and, as a derivative of this orientation, (2) a commitment to build the institutions of civil society by constructing the ecological space for individual citizens to promote in their community institutions of social justice, equity, and democracy. Thus, if young people understand themselves as morally committed to and behaviorally engaged in building civil society, and if as a consequence they possess a transcendent sense of the importance in life of commitment to an enduring nature or being beyond the limits of their own existence, then they can be agents both in their own, healthy development and in the positive enhancement of other people and society.

Given the crucial role of an integrated moral and civic identity and a spiritual sense in the thriving of youth and their communities, it is critical to align public policy and community action (for example, community-based, youth-serving programs) in support of developing such identity. One model for designing the person-context system through which such development occurs involves pursuing a vision of family-centered community building.[78] The family-centered community-building model suggests that our nation can create a developmental system across generations that builds integrated moral and civic identity in its citizens.[79] Such citizens sustain and enhance the institutions of civil society.

Policies can be developed to enhance in the community the capacity of families to generate the individual and ecological assets suggested by Search Institute.[80] Within such a policy context, an asset-rich community enacts activities (programs) that give young people the resources needed to build and pursue healthy lives that make a productive contribution to self, family, and community. Such resources include a healthy start, a safe environment, education for marketable skills, the opportunity to give back to or serve the community, and freedom from prejudice and discrimination.[81]

Thriving is likely to emerge when youth develop in a context of such a policy and community action program.[82] Competent, confident, connected, caring youth who also possess character have the moral orientation and the civic allegiance to use their skills to enact in themselves (and, if a parent, promote in their children) behaviors that level the playing field for all individuals. Committed—behaviorally, morally, and spiritually—to a better world beyond themselves, they act to sustain for future generations a society marked by social justice, equity, and democracy and a world wherein all young people may thrive.

Notes

1. Benson, P. L. (1997a). *All kids are our kids: What communities must do to raise caring and responsible children and adolescents.* San Francisco: Jossey-Bass; Benson, P. L. (in press). Developmental assets, community building, and positive youth development. In R. M. Lerner & P. L. Benson (Eds.), *Developmental assets and asset-building communities: Implications for research, policy, and practice.* Norwell, MA: Kluwer; Benson, P. L., & Pittman, K. J. (Eds.). (2001). *Trends in youth development: Visions, realities and challenges.* Norwell, MA: Kluwer; Benson, P. L., & Saito, R. N. (2001). The scientific foundations of youth development. In P. L. Benson & K. J. Pittman (Eds.), *Trends in youth development.* Norwell, MA: Kluwer; Damon, W. (1997). *The youth charter: How communities can work together to raise standards for all our children.* New York: Free Press; Damon, W., & Gregory, A. (in press). Bringing in a new era in the field of youth development. In Lerner & Benson; Roth, J., Brooks-Gunn, J., Murray, L., & Foster, W. (1998). Promoting healthy adolescents: Synthesis of youth development program evaluations. *Journal of Research on Adolescence, 8,* 423–459.

2. Pittman, K. (1996, Winter). Community, youth, development: Three goals in search of connection. *New Designs for Youth Development,* 4–8; Pittman, K., Irby, M., & Ferber, T. (2001). Unfinished business: Further reflections on a decade of promoting youth development. In Benson & Pittman; Reese, W., Thorup, C. L., & Gerson, T. K. (in press). An alliance for youth development: Second generation models on inter-sectoral partnering (ISP). In D. Wertlieb, F. Jacobs, & R. M. Lerner (Eds.), *Promoting positive youth and family development: Community systems, citizenship, and civil society.* Vol. 3 of R. M. Lerner, F.

Jacobs, & D. Wertlieb (Eds.), *Handbook of applied developmental science: Promoting positive child, adolescent, and family development through research, policies, and programs.* Thousand Oaks, CA: Sage; Wheeler, W. (2000). Emerging organizational theory and the youth development organization. *Applied Developmental Science, 4,* Supplement 1, 47–54.

3. Cummings, E. (in press). Foreword. In Wertlieb, Jacobs, & Lerner; Gore, A. (in press). Foreword. In Lerner &Benson; Kennedy, E. M. (1999). University-community partnerships: A mutually beneficial effort to aid community development and improve academic learning opportunities. *Applied Developmental Science, 3*(4), 197–198.

4. Benson (1997a); Benson (in press); Benson, P. L. (1990). The troubled journey: A portrait of 6th-12th grade youth. Minneapolis: Search Institute.

5. Roth, Brooks-Gunn, Murray, & Foster (1998); Pittman (1996); Pittman, Irby, & Ferber (2001); Little, R. R. (1993). What's working for today's youth: The issues, the programs, and the learnings. Paper presented at ICYF Fellows Colloquium, Michigan State University; Little, R. R. (2000). Personal communication.

6. Damon (1997); Damon, W. (1990). The moral child. New York: Free Press; Youniss, J., & Yates, M. (1999). Youth service and moral-civic identity. A case for everyday morality. *Educational Psychology Review, 11,* 361–376.

7. Flanagan, C., & Faison, N. (2001). Youth civic engagement: Implications of research for social policy and programs. *Social Policy Reports,* No. 1; Flanagan, C., & Sherrod, L. (Eds.). (1998). Political development: Youth growing up in a global community. *Journal of Social Issues, 54*(entire issue 3); Lerner, R. M., Fisher, C. B., & Weinberg, R. A. (2000). Toward a science for and of the people: Promoting civil society through the application of developmental science. *Child Development, 71,* 11–20; Yates, M., & Youniss, J. (1996). Community service and political-moral identity in adolescents. *Journal of Research on Adolescence, 6*(3), 271–284; Youniss, J., Yates, M., & Su, Y. (1997). Social integration: Community service and marijuana use in high school seniors. *Journal of Adolescent Research, 12*(2), 245–262.

8. Bornstein, H. H., Davidson, L., Keyes, C. M., Moore, K. (Eds.), & Center for Child Well-Being. (in press). *Well-being: Positive development across the life course.* Mahwah, NJ: Erlbaum.

9. Scales, P., Benson, P., Leffert, N., & Blyth, D. A. (2000). The contribution of developmental assets to the prediction of thriving among adolescents. *Applied Developmental Science, 4,* 27–46.

10. Lerner, R. M. (2002). *Concepts and theories of human development* (3rd ed.). Mahwah, NJ: Erlbaum.

11. Lerner (2002).

12. Hall, G. (1904). *Adolescence.* New York: Appleton.

13. Roth, Brooks-Gunn, Murray, and Foster (1998).

14. Lerner (2002); Overton, W. F. (1998). Developmental psychology: Philosophy, concepts, and methodology. In R. M. Lerner (Ed.). *Theoretical models of human development: Vol. 1. The handbook of child psychology* (5th ed., pp. 107–189; W. Damon, ed. in chief). New York: Wiley.

15. Lerner (2002); Overton (1998); Gottlieb, G. (1997). *Synthesizing nature-nurture: Prenatal roots of instinctive behavior.* Mahwah, NJ: Erlbaum.

16. Bowlby, J. (1969). *Attachment and loss: Vol. 1. attachment.* New York: Basic Books.

17. Lorenz, K. (1965). *Evolution and modification of behavior.* Chicago: University of Chicago.

18. Plomin, R. (2000). Behavioural genetics in the 21st century. *International Journal of Behavioral Development, 24,* 30–34.

19. Freud, S. (1954). *Collected works* (standard ed.). London: Hogarth.

20. Freud, A. (1969). Adolescence as a developmental disturbance. In G. Caplan and S. Lebovier (Eds.), *Adolescence* (pp. 5–10). New York: Basic Books; Erikson, E. H. (1968). *Identity, youth and crisis.* New York: Norton.

21. Bijou, S. W., and Baer, D. M. (Eds.) (1961). *Child development: A systematic and empirical theory.* New York: Appleton-Century-Crofts.

22. Piaget, J. (1970). Piaget's theory. In P. H. Mussen (Ed.), *Carmichael's Manual of Child Psychology* (pp. 703–732). New York: Wiley.

23. Overton (1998).

24. Ibid.

25. Damon, W. (Ed.). (1998). *Handbook of child psychology* (5th ed.). New York: Wiley

26. Lerner (2002); Overton (1998); Gottlieb (1997); Damon (1998); Ford, D. L., and Lerner, R. M. (1992). *Developmental systems theory: An integrative approach.* Thousand Oaks, CA: Sage; Thelen, E., & Smith, L. B. (1998). Dynamic systems theories. In W. Damon (Series Ed.) & R. M. Lerner (Vol. Ed.), *Handbook of child psychology: Vol. 1. Theoretical models of human development* (5th ed., pp. 563–633). New York: Wiley; Wapner, S., and Demick, J. (1998). Developmental analysis: A holistic, developmental, systems-oriented perspective. In Damon & Lerner (pp. 761–805).

27. Lerner (2002).

28. Lerner (2002); Baltes, P. B., Lindenberger, U., & Staudinger, U. M. (1998). Life-span theory in developmental psychology. In Damon & Lerner (pp. 1029–1144); Lerner, R. M. (1984). *On the nature of human plasticity.* New York: Cambridge.

29. Lerner (2002); Birkel, R., Lerner, R. M., & Smyer, M. A. (1989). Applied developmental psychology as an implementation of a life-span view of human development. *Journal of Applied Developmental Psychology, 10,* 425–445; Fisher, C. B., and Lerner, R. M. (1994). Foundations of applied developmental psychology. In C. B. Fisher and R. M. Lerner (Eds.), *Applied developmental psychology* (pp. 3–20). New York: McGraw-Hill; Lerner, R. M., & Hood, K. E. (1986). Plasticity in development: Concepts and issues for intervention. *Journal of Applied Developmental Psychology, 7,* 139–152.

30. Csikszentmihalyi, M., & Rathunde, K. (1998). The development of the person: An experiential perspective on the ontogenesis of psychological complexity. In Damon & Lerner (pp. 635–684).

31. Benson, P. L. (1997b). Spirituality and the adolescent journey. *Reclaiming Children and Youth, 5*(4), 206–209; Benson, P. L., Masters, K. S., & Larson, D. B. (1997). Religious influences on child and adolescent development. In N. E. Alessi (Ed.), *Handbook of child and adolescent psychiatry* (Vol. 4, pp. 206–219). New York: Wiley.

32. Youniss & Yates (1999); Erikson (1968); Erikson, E. H. (1959). Identity and the life-cycle. *Psychological Issues, 1,* 18–164; Youniss, J., McLellan, J. A., & Yates, M. (1999). Religion, community service, and identity in American youth. *Journal of Adolescence, 22,* 243–253.

33. Camino, L. (2000). Youth-adult partnerships: Entering new territory in community work and research. *Applied Developmental Science, 4,* Supplement 1, 11–20.

34. Zeldin, S., Camino, L., & Wheeler, W. (Eds.). (2000). Promoting adolescent development in community context: Challenges to scholars, nonprofit managers, and higher education. *Applied Developmental Science, 4,* entire Supplement 1.

35. Ford & Lerner (1992); Schneirla, T. C. (1957). The concept of development in comparative psychology. In D. B. Harris (Ed.), *The concept of development* (pp. 78–108). Minneapolis: University of Minnesota; Tobach, E. (1981). Evolutionary aspects of the activity of the organism and its development. In R. M. Lerner and N. A. Busch-Rossnagel (Eds.), *Individuals as producers of their development: A life-span perspective* (pp. 37–68). New York: Academic Press.

36. Bronfenbrenner, U. (1979) *The ecology of human development: Experiments by nature and design.* Cambridge: Harvard University Press; Riegel, K. F. (1975). Toward a dialectical theory of development. *Human Development, 18,* 50–64.

37. Lerner (2002); Overton (1998); Bronfenbrenner, U. (2001). Human development, bioecological theory of. In N. J. Smelser & P. B. Baltes (Eds.), *International encyclopedia of the social and behavioral sciences* (pp. 6963–6970). Oxford: Elsevier.

38. O'Connell, B. (1999). *Civil society: The underpinnings of American democracy.* Hanover, NH: University Press of New England.

39. Lerner (2002); Gould, S. (1977). *Ontogeny and phylogeny.* Cambridge, MA: Harvard University Press; Johanson, D. C., & Edey, M. A. (1981). *Lucy: The beginnings of humankind.* New York: Simon & Schuster.

40. Ibid.; Fisher, H. E. (1982). *Of human bonding. Sciences, 22,* 18ff.

41. Johanson & Edey (1981).

42. Gould (1977).

43. Fisher (1982).

44. Lerner (2002); Ford & Lerner (1992); Lerner, R. M., & Spanier, G. B. (1980). *Adolescent development: A life-span perspective.* New York: McGraw-Hill.

45. Csikszentmihalyi & Rathunde (1998).

46. Ford & Lerner (1992); Elder, G. H., Jr. (1998). The life course and human development. In Damon & Lerner (pp. 939–991).

47. Elder (1998).

48. Brandtstädter, J. (1998). Action perspectives on human development. In Damon & Lerner (pp. 807–863); Heckhausen, J. (1999). *Developmental regulation in adulthood: Age-normative and sociocultural constraints as adaptive challenges.* New York: Cambridge University Press.

49. Elder (1998).

50. Csikszentmihalyi and Rathunde (1998); Erikson (1959).

51. Erikson (1959); Elder, G. H., Modell, J., & Parke, R. D. (1993). Studying children in a changing world. In G. H. Elder, J. Modell, & R. D. Parke (Eds.), *Children in time and place: Developmental and historical insights* (pp. 3–21). New York: Cambridge University Press.

52. Meyer, J. W. (1988). The social constructs of the psychology of childhood: Some contemporary processes. In E. M. Hetherington, R. M. Lerner,

& M. Perlmutter (Eds.), *Child development in life-span perspective* (pp. 47–65). Mahwah, NJ: Erlbaum.

53. Elder, Modell, & Parke (1993).

54. Benson (1997a).

55. O'Connell (1999).

56. Lerner, R. M., Bornstein, M. H., & Smith C. (in press). Child well-being: From elements to integrations. In Bornstein, Davidson, Keyes, Moore (Eds.), & Center for Child Well-Being.

57. Csikszentmihalyi and Rathunde (1998).

58. Roth, Brooks-Gunn, Murray, & Foster (1998); Lerner, Fisher, & Weinberg (2000).

59. Little (2000); Youniss & Yates (1999); Youniss, McLellan, & Yates (1999).

60. Youniss & Yates (1999).

61. Benson (1997b); Benson, Masters, & Larson (1997).

62. Erikson (1959, 1968).

63. Youniss, McLellan, & Yates (1999).

64. Erikson (1959, 1968).

65. Ibid.

66. Lerner & Spanier (1980).

67. Youniss, McLellan, & Yates (1999).

68. Benson (1997b); Benson, Masters, & Larson (1997).

69. Youniss & Yates (1999); Youniss, McLellan, & Yates (1999).

70. Benson (1997b); Benson, Masters, & Larson (1997); Youniss, McLellan, & Yates (1999).

71. Baltes, Lindenberger, & Staudinger (1998); Baltes, P. B., & Baltes, M. M. (1990). Psychological perspectives on successful aging: The model of selective optimization with compensation. In P. B. Baltes & M. M. Baltes (Eds.), *Successful aging: Perspectives from the behavioral sciences* (pp. 1–34). New York: Cambridge University Press.

72. Lerner, Fisher, & Weinberg (2000); Lerner (2002).

73. Lerner, R. M., & Busch-Rossnagel, N. A. (Eds.). (1981). *Individuals as producers of their development: A life-span perspective.* New York: Academic Press; Lerner, R. M., & Walls, T. (1999). Revisiting individuals as producers of their development: From dynamic interactionism to developmental systems. In J. Brandtstädter & R. M. Lerner (Eds.), *Action and self-development: Theory and research through the life-span* (pp. 3–36). Thousand Oaks, CA: Sage.

74. Benson (1997a); Scales, Benson, Leffert, & Blyth (2000); Benson, P. L., Leffert, N., Scales, P. C., & Blyth, D. A. (1998). Beyond the "village" rhetoric: Creating healthy communities for children and adolescents. *Applied Developmental Science, 2*(3), 138–159; Leffert, N., Benson, P. L., Scales, P. C., Sharma, A. R., Drake, D. R., & Blyth, D. A. (1998). Developmental assets: Measurement and prediction of risk behaviors among adolescents. *Applied Developmental Science, 2*, 209–230.

75. Damon (1997); Damon & Gregory (in press).

76. Erikson (1959).

77. Lerner & Spanier (1980); Lerner, R. M., Freund, A. M., De Stefanis, I., & Habermas, T. (2001). Understanding developmental regulation in adoles-

cence: The use of the selection, optimization, and compensation model. *Human Development, 44*, 29–50.

78. Cummings (in press).

79. Gore (in press).

80. Benson (1997a); Benson (in press); Benson, Leffert, Scales, & Blyth (1998); Lerner, Freund, De Stefanis, & Habermas (2001).

81. Lerner, Freund, De Stefanis, & Habermas (2001).

82. Benson & Pittman (2001); Roth, Brooks-Gunn, Murray, & Foster (1998); Pittman, Irby, & Ferber (2001); Lerner, Freund, De Stefanis, & Habermas (2001).

RICHARD M. LERNER *is the Bergstrom Chair in Applied Developmental Science in the Eliot-Pearson Department of Child Development at Tufts University.*

CORNELIA BRENTANO *is research assistant professor in the Eliot-Pearson Department of Child Development.*

ELIZABETH M. DOWLING *is a doctoral student in the Eliot-Pearson Department of Child Development.*

PAMELA M. ANDERSON *is a doctoral student in the Eliot-Pearson Department of Child Development*

An analysis is presented of the longitudinal stability over the course of a year of characteristics of positive functioning and of individual and ecological developmental assets, among African American male youth involved in gangs or in community-based organizations (CBOs) serving youth. Evidence is provided for the potential of positive youth development among both groups of adolescents.

2

Stability of attributes of positive functioning and of developmental assets among African American adolescent male gang and community-based organization members

Carl S. Taylor, Richard M. Lerner,
Alexander von Eye, Aida Bilalbegovic Balsano,
Elizabeth M. Dowling, Pamela M. Anderson,
Deborah L. Bobek, Dragana Bjelobrk

Note: This research was supported in part by a grant from the W. T. Grant Foundation. Further information about this research can be obtained either from Carl S. Taylor, Institute for Children, Youth, and Families, 27 Kellogg Center, Michigan State University, East Lansing, MI 48824; or from Richard M. Lerner, Eliot-Pearson Department of Child Development, 105 College Avenue, Tufts University, Medford, MA 02155.

DEVELOPMENTAL SYSTEMS MODELS pertinent to understanding the characteristics of resiliency among, or the "adaptive modes" used by, adolescents of color and their families, especially in economically poor communities,[1] emphasize that all youth living in these settings have individual and contextual assets that may be used to promote positive behavior and development. This focus on positive youth development among poor youth of color leads to an interest in identifying the individual and ecological characteristics that may result in healthy outcomes even among individuals involved in many of the high-risk behaviors linked to poverty.[2] The study from which this article is derived is framed by this perspective about positive youth development.

"Overcoming the Odds" (OTO) is a longitudinal study of the nature of positive functioning, and of the role of individual and ecological developmental assets in this functioning, among African American male adolescent youth involved either in urban, inner-city gangs or in community-based organizations (CBOs) designed to promote positive youth development.[3] Initial reports from the OTO data set indicate that at the initial wave of data collection (in 1999, when youths in both groups ranged in age from fourteen to eighteen years), the African American male adolescent gang and CBO youth were significantly distinct in regard to both the evidence they showed of positive functioning and their assets for positive development.

Taylor and colleagues[4] reported that among the forty-five African American gang members and the fifty African American CBO youths who participated in the interviews used to collect OTO data, the groups differed in regard to positive attribute scores pertaining to parents and family, peer relations, school and education, drug use, sexual activity, religious activities and religiosity, racial or ethnic identity, role models and confidants, and neighborhood and safety. The correlations among attribute scores were more often significant (that is, "coupled") among the gang than among the CBO youth. However, consistent with the idea that all young people have resources pertinent to positive development, and that therefore gang and nongang youth would have some resource comparability, across the nine attributes about one quarter of the gang youth had total positive attribute scores at the initial point of assessment in OTO that were above the average total positive attribute score among the CBO youth.

Similarly, Taylor, and colleagues[5] assessed the presence of individual and ecological assets for positive development among the two groups of OTO participants. Again, as expected, the CBO youth had a higher level of both asset domains. The African American male adolescent gang and CBO youth were significantly distinct in regard to assets of positive development associated with boundaries and expectations, constructive use of time, support, social competencies, empowerment, commitment to learning, and positive values. However, as occurred in regard to scores for positive functioning, Taylor and colleagues[6] found that the contrast in assets between the gang and CBO youth was not absolute. All gang members possessed at least one asset, and across the seven asset categories studied in OTO 15.6 percent of them had total mean asset scores at the first wave of testing that were more positive than the average total asset score among the CBO youth.

Together, the data from the first wave of testing in OTO are consistent with the scholarship of McAdoo,[7] Spencer,[8] Benson,[9] and Taylor[10]: *all* youth have individual and ecological resources that may be linked to positive development and, as such, that strength-building interventions can capitalize on. This viewpoint is consistent with theory[11] and qualitative research[12] about African American adolescent male gang members. This literature indicates not only the unsurprising differences between gang and CBO adolescents but as well the comparability in family, teacher, and peer resources for positive development between at least some gang members (about 20 percent[13]) and their CBO counterparts.

The data from this first wave of assessment of the OTO sample indicate that there are a subset of gang youth who—despite being embedded in a behavioral and social milieu marked by risks (gang violence, drugs, poor familial support) that transcend the "ambient" problems of poverty and racism—show some characteristics of positive development and possess individual and ecological assets that are linked to their positive functioning. Of course, before one concludes that such strengths remain a significant part of the developmental system for either gang or CBO youth, the longitudinal stability of assets and positive functioning must be ascertained.

Do the strengths present among the gang youth show patterns of constancy comparable to those in evidence for CBO youth? If the strengths of the former proved to be more ephemeral, then a theoretical question would arise in regard to the conditions in the developmental system that constituted a basis for such discontinuity among these groups of young people. As well, program design and policy planning would differ in the face of variation in the stability or instability of trajectories of positive functioning and of the presence of developmental assets. Moreover, to the extent that being embedded in an asset-rich community context promotes positive developmental trajectories,[14] gang and CBO youth who possessed more developmental assets at the initial wave of testing in OTO should show evidence of more positive change than is the case for youth who possessed fewer assets at initial assessment. In the case of the gang youth, such change would be evidence of their "overcoming the odds."

Accordingly, we set three goals. First, we sought to test theoretical ideas about the nature of positive youth development within the person-context developmental system. The second goal was to bring data to bear on the notion that all young people possess attributes that may be associated with positive development and that such development is furthered by development within a community setting possessing key assets for healthy growth. The third goal was to create an empirical base for discussion of the programs and policies that should be designed to enhance positive development among gang youth. As such, we sought to ascertain whether the groups of gang and community-based organization (CBO) adolescent males showed stability over the course of a year in their individual and ecological developmental assets and in their scores for positive individual and social functioning. In addition, we sought to identify whether, particularly among the gang youth, there was any association between longitudinal change (for example, deviation above or below the mean stability of the group) and positive functioning or developmental assets. The goal of these analyses of the relative stability of the groups was to discern if some gang youth showed evidence of overcoming the odds.

It is important to emphasize that our analyses were not directed to documenting that the CBO youth had higher scores for positive functioning or more developmental assets. Both our prior research with these youth[15] and the independent literature[16] document such differences. Rather, the purpose of the present analyses was to see if evidence existed that gang youth with more developmental assets had a significantly greater likelihood to show instability in the direction of gains in positive development than was the case for gang youth with fewer developmental assets.

Method

Details of the method used in OTO have been presented elsewhere in work by Taylor and colleagues.[17] This article summarizes the information.

Sample

Participants in the Overcoming the Odds project were recruited from among the adolescents involved in Taylor's Michigan Gang Research Project (MGRP),[18] an ongoing ethnographic field research project with male and female adolescent gang members in Detroit. The gang members (n = 45) participating in OTO have been involved in their respective gangs for five to ten years. These youth were in their gangs throughout participation in the MGRP; involvement ranged from five to twelve years. All gang members volunteered to take part in the OTO study. Recruitment of the community-based organization (CBO) youth (n = 50) occurred through contacts with community members participating in the

MGRP. All CBO youth volunteered as well. Those in the CBO group had never been part of a gang and have been involved in the MGRP for the same range of time as have the gang members. The CBO youth participated in at least one of several CBOs designed to promote positive youth development (such as a church group, 4-H club, or MGRP activity conducted by Taylor[19]).

In both the gang and the CBO groups, most youth were between fourteen and eighteen years of age at the initial wave of testing (April and May 1999; mean ages = 15.82 and 16.31 years, respectively). The second wave of testing occurred one year after the initial wave, in April and May 2000. The age distribution among the adolescents in the gang group was somewhat younger than that in the CBO group, $\chi^2 (8) = 18.4$, $p < .05$. In both groups, the majority were born in Detroit; however, significantly more CBO participants lived with their parents than was the case with the gang members, $\chi^2 (5) = 16.9$, $p < .01$. In addition, the groups differed significantly in regard to parental education, $\chi^2 (5) = 21.9$, $p < .001$. The CBO youth were more likely to have parents who completed high school or some other type of school, while the gang youth were more likely to report that their parents did not complete any school. Both the gang and CBO youth were either students in or, had they attended school, would have been students in one of twenty schools located within the boundaries of the city of Detroit.

Interview method

Consistent with the methodological recommendations of Joe[20] and of Valdez and Kaplan,[21] Taylor's methods[22] rely centrally on being part of and serving the community. As underscored by Joe[23] and Valdez and Kaplan,[24] the ethnographic interview methods used by Taylor[25] are needed because many of the participants, regardless of the nature of their gang membership or affiliation with another community group, will not respond in writing to a questionnaire. To maximize their willingness to respond to the interview questions, the young people have a "gatekeeper" option: they may participate in group interviews (with their gang leaders present). In the first wave of data in OTO, 100 percent of the CBO youth participated in individual interviews, and 75 percent of the gang members participated in group interviews.

The interview protocol: Content and coding

The protocol for the OTO interview appears in Taylor and colleagues' work.[26] The protocol contains five items pertaining to demographic information (age, people with whom the participant lives, parents' place of birth, participant's place of birth, and parents' educational level) and thirty-nine substantive items. The substantive items are associated with nine categories: nine parent and family items, two peer relation items, five school and education items, ten drug use items, three sexual activity items, two religious activity and religiosity items, two racial or ethnic identity items, three role model and confidant items, and three neighborhood and safety items.

The *response alternatives* associated with each of the items were placed in a "positive" or a "not positive" category, or—if necessary—a "nonapplicable" (to a positive or not-positive classification) category. In all cases, the positive coding (given a score of 1) was reflective of a basis of a behavioral strength or an instance of healthy functioning on the part of the adolescent. The not-positive and nonapplicable categorizations were given a score of zero. To illustrate, responses of "excellent" or "fair" in regard to the item "How would you rate your relationship with your parents?" could be categorized as positive (and scored as 1), whereas responding to this question with "poor" could be categorized as not positive (and scored as zero). The response "talk it out" to the item "How do you settle disputes between your friends?" could be rated as positive (and scored as 1), whereas the response "fight with fists" or "guns" could be seen as not positive (and scored as zero).

Assessment of interrater agreement in regard to categorizing the response alternatives offered evidence of reliability. A Cohen's kappa of .872 ($p < .001$) was obtained. Disagreements were resolved by consensus. Because the raters agreed that three of the eligible questions could not be scored in agreement, the final scoring included thirty-six questions.

In addition to using the questionnaire to code for the presence of positive attributes in the *responses* of the participants, Taylor and colleagues[27] demonstrated that the *questions* in the interview could be related to the model of developmental assets devised by Benson and his colleagues.[28] As such, the set of positive responses in regard to asset categories was placed by two expert independent raters into one of the four internal categories of assets of this model, one of the four external categories of assets of this model, or a demographic category.[29]

The raters agreed on thirty-two of the forty-one interview items (78 percent), resulting in a Cohen's kappa of .74 ($p < .001$). Only those items for which there was agreement between the two expert raters were classified into the asset categories. Six of the items on which the raters agreed were demographic, and one item they agreed on was not applicable to an asset category. The remaining twenty-five items related to an asset category. No item was placed into the positive identity asset category, and one item ("Do your parents use legal drugs?") was placed into an asset category; but the responses to this question could not be scored into positive or not positive. As such, a final set of twenty-four items remained in the pool of "indirectly measured" developmental assets.

Procedure

The two waves of data collection in OTO completed to date occurred in April and May 1999 and April and May 2000. At each wave, the interview was administered to both groups of participants. No attrition occurred across the two waves. For both waves of data collection, all interviews were conducted in a setting selected by the youth (a gang or CBO meeting area, a public location such as a restaurant, or the home of the participant or a friend or relative).

Results

The purpose of this study was to ascertain whether the groups of adolescent males in gangs or community-based organizations

showed stability over the course of a year in their individual and ecological developmental assets and in their scores for positive individual and social functioning. In addition, we sought to identify whether
(particularly among the gang youth) there was any association
between type of longitudinal change and characteristics associated
with positive functioning or developmental assets. That is, our analyses of the relative stability of the groups were aimed at specifying if
some gang youth showed evidence of overcoming the odds.

Stability may be indexed in several ways. For example, nomo-
thetically speaking, stability may be appraised through analysis of
mean changes over time, by appraisal of intravariable, cross-time
correlation, and by assessment of the consistency over time of
intervariable relations. Idiographically, stability may be indexed,
for instance, by ipsative changes in the intraindividual ordering of
variables (say, from most to least positive) or by appraisal of individual growth curves. All these approaches to stability analysis
were pursued.

Group analyses

Nomothetic data treatment methods focus on analyzing group
data. The results of this type of analysis are reported in this section. Table 2.1 presents for the gang and CBO youth the means
and standard deviations associated at each time of measurement
with each of the nine categories of positive functioning (and with
the total score for such functioning) and with each of the seven
categories of developmental assets (and with the total asset
score).

As noted in the table, and as explained in the method section,
the categories of positive functioning pertained to such domains
as family, peers, identity, and sexuality. The categories of developmental assets reflected dimensions of individual functioning
and the social context that reflect "psychosocial" nutrients for
healthy development, such as support, empowerment, and positive values.

Through the use of two MANOVAs—involving in each case a
2 (group) × 2 (time), between-within, mixed-model analysis,

Table 2.1. Means and standard deviations at the two times of measurement for positive functioning and developmental assets

| | Gang Youths | | CBO Youths | |
Scores for:	Time 1 Mean (SD)	Time 2 Mean (SD)	Time 1 Mean (SD)	Time 2 Mean (SD)
Attributes of positive functioning:				
1. Family	4.04 (3.18)	3.84 (3.07)	6.98 (1.52)	6.94 (1.53)
2. Drug use	1.96 (1.45)	1.93 (1.47)	2.58 (1.55)	2.66 (1.55)
3. Peers	.98 (.62)	.89 (.57)	1.54 (.61)	1.58 (.61)
4. School and education	1.93 (1.91)	1.84 (1.91)	3.96 (1.19)	3.88 (1.21)
5. Religiosity	.38 (.72)	.36 (.71)	1.08 (.78)	1.08 (.78)
6. Racial identity	1.47 (.63)	1.40 (.62)	1.82 (.39)	1.78 (.42)
7. Neighborhood and safety	.67 (.85)	.58 (.84)	1.30 (.95)	1.30 (.93)
8. Sexual activity	.56 (.66)	.58 (.58)	1.18 (.66)	1.14 (.64)
9. Role models	1.53 (.87)	1.60 (.86)	2.58 (.54)	2.64 (.53)
Total score	13.51 (8.50)	13.02 (8.21)	23.02 (4.88)	23.00 (4.71)
Developmental assets:				
1. Support	3.51 (2.02)	3.53 (1.96)	5.50 (1.28)	5.44 (1.34)
2. Empowerment	.31 (.47)	.27 (.45)	.60 (.67)	.60 (.64)
3. Boundaries and expectations	3.20 (2.13)	3.16 (2.03)	4.80 (1.50)	4.90 (1.50)
4. Constructive use of time	.38 (.72)	.36 (.71)	1.08 (.78)	1.08 (.78)
5. Commitment to learning	.56 (.69)	.53 (.66)	1.56 (.61)	1.50 (.61)
6. Positive values	.27 (.45)	.20 (.40)	.38 (.49)	.36 (.48)
7. Social competencies	.84 (.64)	.71 (.59)	1.62 (.57)	1.60 (.57)
Total score	9.07 (5.60)	8.76 (5.24)	15.54 (3.66)	15.48 (3.58)

Note: n = 45 for gang youths; n = 50 for CBO youths

wherein the scores for positive functioning and for developmental assets served as the vector of dependent variables, respectively— evidence was found that CBO youth had higher positive attribute scores, $F(1, 93) = 50.95$, $p < .001$; and higher asset scores, $F(1, 93) = 51.17$, $p < .001$, than did the gang youth. However, and indicative of mean-level group stability, there was no significant time or group $\times$ time interaction for either the attribute scores or the asset scores.

Time 1–time 2 Pearson product-moment correlations were computed among all nine positive attribute scores and the total attribute score, and separately among all seven developmental asset scores and the total asset score, for the gang members and the CBO youth. For the former, these time 1–time 2 autocorrelations for the nine attribute scores and for the total attribute score ranged from .66 (for "peers") to .98 (for "drug use"); the average autocorrelation was .90. Among the CBO youth, these autocorrelations ranged from .86 (for "sexual activity") to 1.0 (for "religiosity"); the average autocorrelation was .96. Moreover, all but one of the one hundred correlations for the gang youth and all but two of the hundred correlations for the CBO youth in the matrix of intercorrelations among the ten attribute scores were positive. In addition, a significantly higher proportion of the correlations were significant ($p < .05$) among the gang youth (that is, 84 percent) than among the CBO group (that is, 46 percent).

Similar correlational findings were obtained in regard to the developmental asset scores. For the gang participants, these time 1–time 2 autocorrelations for the seven developmental asset scores and for the total asset score ranged from .60 (for "social competencies") to .98 (for "commitment to learning"); the average autocorrelation was .89. Among the CBO participants, these autocorrelations ranged from .87 (for both "commitment to learning" and "positive values") to 1.0 for ("constructive use of time"); the average autocorrelation was .96. Moreover, for both groups, all of the sixty-four correlations in the matrix of intercorrelations among the eight asset scores were positive. In addition, a significantly higher proportion of the correlations were significant

($p < .05$) among the gang youth (80 percent) than among the CBO youth (55 percent).

As did the analyses of mean changes over time, these correlational analyses indicated that both groups showed comparable patterns of autocorrelational stability for the attribute and developmental asset scores. However, both sets of scores were more often significantly interrelated over time among the gang youth. Thus, as reported by Taylor and colleagues,[30] attributes of positive functioning and indicators of developmental assets are more highly coupled among gang members than among CBO youth.

We next computed for each gang and CBO youth the time 1–time 2 differences for each of his ten attribute and eight developmental asset scores. We then computed the Pearson product-moment correlations among these difference (change) scores and the positive attribute and developmental asset scores each youth attained at the second time of testing. These analyses allowed us to identify whether there was an association between magnitude of longitudinal change and particular characteristics of positive functioning or developmental assets at the second time of measurement.[31]

There was little evidence for association. Generally, for neither gang nor CBO youth was the time 1–time 2 difference for any attribute or asset score correlated with higher time 2 scores. Of the one hundred correlations for the gang youth between time 1–time 2 differences in positive attributes and attribute scores at time 2, 6 percent were significant (four were positive and two were negative), and in turn, of the sixty-four correlations for this group time 1–time 2 differences in developmental assets and time 2 asset scores 6.3 percent were significant (two were positive and two were negative). Similarly, of the one hundred correlations for the CBO youth between time 1–time 2 differences in positive attributes and attribute scores at time 2, 4 percent were significant (one was positive and three were negative), and in turn, of the sixty-four correlations for this group between time 1–time 2 differences in developmental assets and time 2 assets, 6.3 percent were significant (one was positive and three were negative).

Thus, even though gang and CBO youth showed comparable levels of mean level and autocorrelational stability in regard to attribute and developmental asset scores, there was little dispersion within or between groups in the type of change and little significant covariation between change type and these two sets of scores. As such, these nomothetic analyses did not yield evidence for overcoming the odds among the gang youth. Accordingly, idiographic analyses were conducted to assess whether patterns of intraindividual change might produce such evidence.

Individual analyses

Idiographic data treatment methods focus on analyzing individual data. For instance, rather than compare a person's score on a given behavioral measure to corresponding scores of other people (as is done in nomothetic analysis), the person's score on a given measure is compared to his or her score on another measure or to his or her score on the given measure at another point in time. Such idiographic procedures are termed ipsative analyses.[32]

Nomothetic analysis of stability need not reflect patterns of change assessed at the level of the individual.[33] Accordingly, to supplement the nomothetic analyses of stability reported here, two approaches to idiographic analysis were pursued. In essence, these procedures move our analytic frame from a quantitative approach to a qualitative one. As such, they enable us to explore whether it is possible to triangulate evidence for overcoming the odds (for plasticity in developmental change) across these distinct methodological frames. Both qualitative approaches we employed involved analysis of ipsative changes.[34] We compared the intraindividual ordering of variables (from most to least positive) at each time of testing completed to date in OTO; as well, we appraised the individual growth curves of the participants for all the positive attribute and developmental asset scores.

Both types of analysis were undertaken to assess whether a young person who changes most in regard to his positive attribute scores was likely, by the end of the one-year assessment period, to show either more developmental assets at time 2 or greater growth in development assets across the two times of measurement. To test these possibilities, the within-participant distribution of positive attribute scores was inspected at each time of testing.

These distributions were treated in two ways. First, at each time of testing the attributes were converted to standard scores and then rank-ordered from highest to lowest among both the gang and CBO youth. Each participant was assigned a score (which could range from zero to 9) for the number of these nine attributes that changed rank-order location. Each participant's intraindividual "rank order change" score was correlated with his total developmental asset score at time 2 and, as well, with the difference score between the total asset scores at times 1 and 2.

Second, each participant was assigned a score (which also could range from zero to 9) for the number of nine attributes whose individual growth curves reflected an increase in positive functioning across the two times of testing. This "growth" score was correlated also with the participant's total developmental asset score at time 2 and, as well, with the difference score between total asset scores at times 1 and 2.

Rank-order changes for the attribute scores ranged from zero to 9 among the gang youth (mean = 4.00, SD = 3.13) and from zero to 9 among the CBO youth (mean = 2.96, SD = 2.59). Similarly, growth scores ranged from 1 to 8 among the gang youth (mean = 5.89, SD =1.37) and from 6 to 8 among the CBO youth (mean = 6.76, SD = .59). Although the groups did not differ in their intraindividual rank-order scores for their positive attributes, t (93) = 1.77, $p < .05$, the CBO youth did display greater growth than gang members in positive attributes, t (93) = 4.10, $p < .001$.

Among the CBO youth, there was no significant covariation between intraindividual rank-order change scores and the total developmental asset score at time 2, r (48) = .21 (n.s.). However, a significant relation existed between the intraindividual growth score and the score for change in developmental assets between time 1 and time 2, r (48) = .57, $p < .01$. In turn, and consistent with the presence of intraindividual change in the direction of positive development—of overcoming the odds—both of the corresponding correlations among the gang members were significant. This is the correlation between intraindividual rank-order change scores and the total developmental asset score at time 2 was $r(43) = .35$, $p < .05$; and the correlation between the intraindividual growth score and the score for change in developmental assets between time 1 and time 2 was $r(43) = .67$, $p < .01$. These correlations provided evidence for the growth of positive functioning among gang youth, functioning that is linked—(at levels comparable to those for the CBO youth) to developmental assets.

In regard to the correlations between the interindividual growth score and the score for change in developmental assets between time 1 and time 2, 75 percent of correlations (six out of eight) were significantly correlated in gang youth, whereas in CBO youth only 25 percent of correlations (two out of eight) were significantly correlated. The difference between these two proportions proved to be significant as well ($z = 2.00$, $p < .05$). Thus, in distinction to the results from nomothetic analysis, idiographic analysis afforded evidence that when gang youth are linked in their ecologies to developmental assets they have not only developmental plasticity but more specifically the potential for positive development change (that is, for overcoming the odds).

Discussion

The purpose of the OTO project is to test theoretical ideas about the nature of positive youth development within the person-context developmental system.[35] The study is designed to bring longitudinal data to bear on the notion that all young people possess attributes that may be associated with positive development and that it is furthered within a community setting possessing key assets for healthy growth. We believe that such data may constitute an empirical base for discussion of the programs and policies that should be designed to enhance positive development, especially among those youth stereotypically viewed from the vantage point of a deficit model, one wherein young people are seen as possessing a constellation of problems that require, at best, preventive action aimed at problem management.[36] African American gang youth are prototypically placed in such a deficit category; thus the OTO project seeks to ascertain whether gang youth evince the bases of positive development.

The report in this article asks whether gang and CBO adolescent males showed stability over the course of a year in their individual and ecological developmental assets and in their scores for positive individual and social functioning. We sought to identify whether, particularly among the gang youth, there was any association between longitudinal change in positive functioning and the presence of (or change in) developmental assets. The goal of these analyses of the relative stability of the groups was to discern if some gang youth showed evidence of overcoming the odds.

We recognize that the small sample size involved in OTO and the statistical issues entailed in deriving two sets of scores (positive attributes and developmental assets) from a common data set impose limitations of the measurement model we used to assess both attributes of positive functioning and developmental assets. Nevertheless, we believe that the results we obtained indicate that the data from the first two waves of assessment of the OTO sample have both basic and applied significance. Substantively, the data reported here suggest that among gang youth there is a link between positive developmental change and developmental assets. Interestingly, this association was identified in person-centered, idiographic (or intraindividual, or ipsative[37]) analysis but was not discernible in variable-focused nomothetic (group) analysis. That is, in nomothetic analysis, both gang and CBO youth showed comparable patterns of mean level and autocorrelational stability for the attribute and developmental asset scores. Moreover, both groups were similar as well in manifesting little dispersion within or between groups in the type of change and the covariation between change types and these two sets of scores. However, as reported by Taylor and colleagues,[38] attributes of positive functioning and indicators of developmental assets are more highly coupled among gang members than among CBO youth.

Although these nomothetic analyses of stability did not produce findings indicative of gang youth overcoming the odds, the results of the idiographic analyses of intraindividual change did present such evidence. Intraindividual analysis of rank-order change in positive attributes and of growth in scores for positive attributes across the two times of testing indicated that intraindividual change was linked among gang youth, more so than among the CBO youth, to developmental assets present at time 2. Consistent with theoretical ideas about the potential for positive youth development among all adolescents, idiographic analysis offered evidence that when gang youth are linked in their ecologies to developmental assets they have not only developmental plasticity but in particular the potential for positive development change, for overcoming the odds.

Although the direction of effect between positive change and assets cannot be determined readily within the constraints of the present data set, this finding nevertheless underscores the point that all groups of young people may possess the basis for positive development[39] and that, accordingly, if individual and ecological conditions are appropriately integrated the basis may be enhanced in regard to providing resources or assets for healthy development.[40] The individual and ecological assets possessed by gang youth may be the appropriate target of community-based efforts aimed at increasing the probability of youth overcoming the odds against them. The data in this report suggest that all gang youth may be seen as possessing one or more assets that are the key to unlocking the potential of their positive development.

How to identify and use this key varies with the individual; thus we do not underestimate the subtlety that must be built into policy and program efforts. However, clarity about what needs to be involved in this individualization of enhancement efforts is improved when the more precise role over time of a gang member's assets of positive development is identified. Accordingly, the strength and importance of this report's interpretations will be clarified as refined measurement models of individual and contextual characteristics are employed over time to appraise the dynamic of individual development within community settings rich in developmental assets for positive youth development.

Notes

1. Luster, T., & McAdoo, H. P. (1994). Factors related to the achievement and adjustment of young African American children. *Child Development, 65,* 1080–1094; Luster, T., & McAdoo, H. (1996). Family and child influences on educational attainment: A secondary analysis of the High/Scope Perry Preschool data. *Developmental Psychology, 32*(1), 26–39; McAdoo, H. P. (1995). Stress levels, family help patterns, and religiosity in middle- and working-class African American single mothers. *Journal of Black Psychology, 21,* 424–449; McAdoo, H. P. (1998). African American families: Strength and realities. In H. C. McCubbin, E. Thompson, & J. Futrell (Eds.), *Resiliency in ethnic minority families: African American families* (pp. 17–30). Thousand Oaks, CA: Sage; McAdoo, H. P. (1999). Diverse children of color. In H. E. Fitzgerald, B. M. Lester, & B. S. Zuckerman (Eds.), *Children of color: Research, health, and policy issues* (pp. 205–218). New York: Garland; Spencer, M. B. (1990). Development of minority children: An introduction. *Child Development, 61,* 267–269; Spencer, M. B. (1995). Old issues and new theorizing about African American youth: A phenomenological variant of ecological systems theory. In R. L. Taylor (Ed.), *Black youth: Perspectives on their status in the United States* (pp. 38–69). Westport, CT: Praeger; Spencer, M. B. (1999). Social and cultural influences on school adjustment: The application of an identity-focused cultural ecological perspective. *Educational Psychologist, 34,* 43–57; Spencer, M. B., Harpalani, V., Fegley, S., Dell'Angelo, T., & Seaton, G. (in press). Identity, self, and peers in context: A culturally-sensitive, developmental framework for analysis. In R. M. Lerner, F. Jacobs, & D. Wertlieb (Eds.), *Applying developmental science for youth and families: Historical and theoretical foundations: Vol. 1. Handbook of applied developmental science: Promoting positive child, adolescent, and family development through research, policies, and programs.* Thousand Oaks, CA: Sage; Spencer, M. B., Dupree, D., & Hartmann, T. (1997). A phenomenological variant of ecological systems theory (PVEST): A self-organization perspective in context. *Development and Psychopathology, 9,* 817–833.

2. Benson, P. (1997). *All kids are our kids: What communities must do to raise caring and responsible children and adolescents.* San Francisco: Jossey-Bass; Benson, P. (in press b). Developmental assets and asset-building communities: Implications for research, policy, and practice. In R. M. Lerner & P. Benson (Eds.), *Developmental assets and asset-building communities: Implications for research, policy, and programs.* Norwell, MA: Kluwer; Benson, P. (in press a). Building communities for healthy youth and families: A vision for the future. In Lerner & Benson; Benson, P. L., & Pittman, K. J. (Eds.). (2001). *Trends in youth development: Visions, realities, and challenges.* Norwell, MA: Kluwer; Dryfoos, J. G. (1990). *Adolescents at risk: Prevalence and prevention.* New York: Oxford University Press; Huston, A. C. (1991). *Children in poverty: Child development and public policy.* Cambridge: Cambridge University Press.

3. Taylor, C. S., Lerner, R. M., von Eye, A., Bobek, D., Balsano, A., Dowling, E., & Anderson, P. M. (in press). Positive individual and social behavior among gang and non-gang African American male adolescents. *Journal of Ado-*

lescent Research; Taylor, C. S., Lerner, R. M., von Eye, A., Bobek, D., Bilalbe-govic Balsano, A., Dowling, E., & Anderson, P. (in press). Internal and external developmental assets among African American male gang members. *Journal of Adolescent Research.*

4. Taylor, Lerner, von Eye, Bobek, Balsano, et al. (in press).

5. Taylor, Lerner, von Eye, Bobek, Bilalbegovic Balsano, et al. (in press).

6. Ibid.

7. Luster & McAdoo (1994); Luster & McAdoo (1996); McAdoo (1995); McAdoo (1998); McAdoo (1999).

8. Spencer (1990); Spencer (1995); Spencer (1999); Spencer, Dupree, & Hartmann (1997).

9. Benson (1997); Benson (in press a); Benson (in press b); Benson & Pittman (2001).

10. Taylor, C. S. (1990). *Dangerous society.* East Lansing: Michigan State University Press; Taylor, C. S. (1993). *Girls, gangs, women, and drugs.* East Lansing: Michigan State University Press; Taylor, C. S. (1996, January). The unintended consequences of incarceration: Youth development, the juvenile corrections systems, and crime. Paper presented at the Vera Institute Conference, Harriman, NY; Taylor, C. S. (2001). Youth gangs. In N. J. Smelser & P. B. Baltes (Eds.), *International encyclopedia of the social and behavioral sciences* (pp. 16664–16668). Oxford: Elsevier.

11. Joe, K. (1993). Issues in accessing and studying ethnic youth gangs. *Journal of Gang Research,* *1*(2), 9–23; Neely, D. E. (1997). The social reality of African American street gangs. *Journal of Gang Research,* *4*(2), 37–46.

12. Patton, P. L. (1998). The gangstas in our midst. *Urban Review,* *30*(1), 49–76. Norwell, MA: Kluwer.

13. Ibid.

14. Benson (in press a); Benson (in press b); Lerner, R. M., & Benson, P. L. (Eds.) (in press). Developmental assets and asset-building communities: Implications for research, policy, and programs. Norwell, MA: Kluwer.

15. Taylor, Lerner, von Eye, Bobek, Balsano, et al. (in press); Taylor, Lerner, von Eye, Bobek, Bilalbegovic Balsano, et al. (in press).

16. Joe (1993); Neely (1997); Valdez, A., & Kaplan, C. D. (1999). Reducing selection bias in the use of focus groups to investigate hidden populations: The case of Mexican-American gang members from south Texas. *Drugs and Society,* *14*(1–2), 209–224.

17. Taylor, Lerner, von Eye, Bobek, Balsano, et al. (in press); Taylor, Lerner, von Eye, Bobek, Bilalbegovic Balsano, et al. (in press).

18. Taylor (1990); Taylor (1993); Taylor (1996); Taylor (2001).

19. Taylor (1993); Taylor (1996).

20. Joe (1993).

21. Valdez & Kaplan (1999).

22. Taylor (1990); Taylor (1993); Taylor (1996); Taylor (2001).

23. Joe (1993).

24. Valdez & Kaplan (1999).

25. Taylor (1990); Taylor (1993); Taylor (1996); Taylor (2001).

26. Taylor, Lerner, von Eye, Bobek, Balsano, et al. (in press).

27. Taylor, Lerner, von Eye, Bobek, Bilalbegovic Balsano, et al. (in press).

28. Benson (1997); Benson, P. L., Leffert, N., Scales, P. C., & Blyth, D. A. (1998). Beyond the "village" rhetoric: Creating healthy communities for children and adolescents. *Applied Developmental Science, 2*(3), 138–159.

29. These raters were Peter Scales and Nancy Leffert, key colleagues in the developmental asset work of Search Institute. See also Leffert, N., Benson, P. L., Scales, P. C., Sharma, A. R., Drake, D. R., and Blyth, D. A. (1998). Developmental assets: Measurement and prediction of risk behaviors among adolescents. *Applied Developmental Science, 2,* 209–230; Scales, P., & Leffert, N. (1999). *Developmental assets: A synthesis of the scientific research on adolescent development.* Minneapolis: Search Institute; and Scales, P., Benson, P., Leffert, N., & Blyth, D. A. (2000). The contribution of developmental assets to the prediction of thriving among adolescents. *Applied Developmental Science, 4*(1), 27–46.

30. Taylor, Lerner, von Eye, Bobek, Balsano, et al. (in press); Taylor, Lerner, von Eye, Bobek, Bilalbegovic Balsano, et al. (in press).

31. We are aware that the search for positive relations through these analyses is constrained by the fact that the largest observations at time 1 can only remain stable or decrease at time 2, whereas the lowest observations at time 1 can only remain stable or increase at time 2; this type of analysis therefore always involves a negative component.

32. Lerner, R. M. (2002). *Concepts and theories of human development* (3rd ed.). Mahwah, NJ: Erlbaum.

33. Ibid.; Werner, H. (1957). The concept of development from a comparative and organismic point of view. In D. B. Harris (Ed.), *The concept of development* (pp. 125–148). Minneapolis: University of Minnesota Press.

34. Lerner (2002).

35. Benson (1997); Benson (in press b); Lerner (2002).

36. Roth, J., Brooks-Gunn, J., Murray, L., & Foster, W. (1998). Promoting healthy adolescents: Synthesis of youth development program evaluations. *Journal of Research on Adolescence, 8,* 423–459.

37. Lerner (2002).

38. Taylor, Lerner, von Eye, Bobek, Balsano, et al. (in press); Taylor, Lerner, von Eye, Bobek, Bilalbegovic Balsano, et al. (in press).

39. McAdoo (1995); McAdoo (1999); Spencer (1990); Spencer (1995); Spencer (1999); Benson (1997); Taylor (1996); Taylor (2001).

40. McAdoo (1995); Spencer (1990); Benson (1997).

CARL S. TAYLOR *is professor in the Department of Family and Child Ecology at Michigan State University.*

RICHARD M. LERNER *is the Bergstrom Chair in Applied Developmental Science in the Eliot-Pearson Department of Child Development at Tufts University.*

ALEXANDER VON EYE *is professor in the Department of Psychology at Michigan State University.*

AIDA BILALBEGOVIC BALSANO, ELIZABETH M. DOWLING, *and* PAMELA M. ANDERSON *are doctoral students in the Eliot-Pearson Department of Child Development at Tufts University.*

DEBORAH L. BOBEK *is managing director of the Applied Developmental Science Institute at Tufts University.*

DRAGANA BJELOBRK *is a doctoral student in the Department of Family and Child Ecology at Michigan State University.*

The Search Institute framework for conceptualizing developmental assets was used in a longitudinal study of African American male youth involved in gangs or in community-based organizations (CBOs) serving youth. Analyses of intraindividual change indicated that individual and ecological assets are linked to positive developmental trajectories among these youth.

3

Individual and ecological assets and positive developmental trajectories among gang and community-based organization youth

Carl S. Taylor, Richard M. Lerner,
Alexander von Eye, Aida Bilalbegovic Balsano,
Elizabeth M. Dowling, Pamela M. Anderson,
Deborah L. Bobek, Dragana Bjelobrk

"OVERCOMING THE ODDS" (OTO) is a longitudinal study of the nature of positive functioning, and of the role of individual and ecological developmental assets in this functioning, among African

Note: this research was supported in part by a grant from the W. T. Grant Foundation. Further information about this research can be obtained either from Carl S. Taylor, Institute for Children, Youth, and Families, 27 Kellogg Center, Michigan State University, East Lansing, MI 48824; or from Richard M. Lerner, Eliot-Pearson Department of Child Development, 105 College Ave., Tufts University, Medford, MA 02155.

NEW DIRECTIONS FOR YOUTH DEVELOPMENT, NO. 95, FALL 2002 © WILEY PERIODICALS, INC.

American male adolescent youth involved either in urban, inner-city gangs or in community-based organizations (CBOs) designed to promote positive youth development.[1] The conceptual frame of OTO is derived from developmental systems theories pertinent to understanding the characteristics of resiliency among, or the "adaptive modes" used by, adolescents of color and their families, especially in economically poor communities.[2]

These theories—for example, the phenomenological variant of ecological systems theory (PVEST) model[3]—emphasize that all youth living in these settings have individual and contextual assets that may be used to promote positive behavior and development. This focus on positive youth development among poor youth of color leads to an interest in identifying the "adaptive modes",[4] or the individual and ecological assets,[5] that may promote positive developmental change even among individuals involved in many of the high risk behaviors linked to poverty.[6]

The data from the first wave of testing in OTO[7] were consistent with the scholarship of McAdoo,[8] Spencer,[9] Benson,[10] and Taylor[11] in offering evidence that all young people possess individual and ecological resources that may be linked to positive development. For instance, the data from this first wave of OTO indicated that there is a subset of gang youth who—despite being embedded in a behavioral and social milieu marked by risks (gang violence, drugs, poor familial support) that transcend the "ambient" problems of poverty and racism—show some characteristics of positive development and possess individual and ecological assets that are linked to their positive functioning. Similarly, in our exploration[12] (Chapter Two of this volume) of whether the gang and CBO adolescent males in OTO showed stability over the course of a year in their individual and ecological developmental assets and in their scores for positive individual and social functioning, we found evidence in idiographic (individual) analyses that some gang members showed evidence of "overcoming the odds."

For instance, through nomothetic (group) analysis we found there was no systematic association between the magnitude of longitudinal change and particular characteristics of positive functioning or developmental assets at a second time of measurement (see Chapter Two). The results of idiographic analysis provided evidence, however, that for gang youth but not for CBO youth a significant relation existed between intraindividual change in positive attributes and developmental assets at a second time of measurement. In addition, intraindividual change in positive attributes was related among gang and CBO youth to change in developmental assets across two times of testing.

This chapter builds on these findings to present more information about the specific individual and ecological assets that are associated with positive developmental trajectories among the gang members and CBO youth. Such information has important theoretical and applied significance. Enhanced knowledge of how particular developmental assets may be linked to longitudinal change in positive development may elucidate understanding of the attractor states that organize the developmental system in adolescence.[13] In turn, this knowledge may guide both policy design and community action strategies in regard to priorities for community building efforts.[14] Accordingly, the idiographic scores for growth in positive functioning were interrelated with the individual and ecological asset scores within and across times of measurement. In addition, using configural frequency analysis techniques,[15] we assessed whether specific combinations of change trajectories and asset scores characterized the gang or the CBO youth.

Method

Details of the method used in OTO have been presented in Chapter Two of this volume and elsewhere.[16] This chapter summarizes the information.

Sample

Participants in the OTO project were volunteers (forty-five gang members and fifty youth from community-based organizations, or

CBOs) from among the adolescents involved in Taylor's Michigan Gang Research Project (MGRP).[17] In both the gang and CBO groups, most youth were between fourteen and eighteen years of age at the initial wave of testing (April and May 1999; mean ages = 15.82 and 16.31 years, respectively). The second wave of testing occurred one year after the initial wave, in April and May 2000. The gang group were somewhat younger than the CBO group, $\chi^2 (8) = 18.4$, $p < .05$. In both, the majority of the youth were born in Detroit. More CBO youth lived with their parents than was the case with the gang members, $\chi^2 (5) = 16.9$, $p < .01$; the CBO youth were more likely to have parents who completed high school or some other type of school, while the gang members were more likely to report that their parents did not complete any school, $\chi^2 (5) = 21.9$, $p < .001$.

The interview protocol: Content and coding

The protocol for the OTO interview appears in work by Taylor and colleagues.[18] To maximize their willingness to respond to the interview questions, youth have a "gatekeeper" option; that is, they may participate in group interviews (with their gang leaders present). In the first wave of data in OTO, 100 percent of the CBO youth participated in individual interviews, and 75 percent of the gang members participated in group interviews. The interview protocol contains five demographic items (age, people with whom the participant lives, parents' place of birth, participant's place of birth, and parents' educational level) and thirty-nine substantive items associated with nine categories: parent and family (nine items), peer relations (two), school and education (five), drug use (ten), sexual activity (three), religious activities and religiosity (two), racial or ethnic identity (two), role models and confidants (three), and neighborhood and safety (three).

The *response alternatives* associated with each item were placed into either a "positive" or a "not positive" category, or—if necessary—a "nonapplicable" (to a positive or not-positive classification) category. In all cases, the positive coding (given a score of 1) was reflective of a basis of a behavioral strength or an instance of healthy functioning on the part of the adolescent. The not-positive and nonapplicable categorizations were given a score of zero. To illustrate, responses of "excellent" or "fair" in regard to the item "How would you rate your relationship with your parents?" could be categorized as positive (and scored as 1), whereas a response to this question of "poor" could be categorized as not positive (and scored as zero).

Assessment of interrater agreement in regard to categorizing the response alternatives gave evidence of reliability (Cohen's kappa = .872, p <.001). Disagreement was resolved by consensus. Because the raters agreed that three of the eligible questions could not be scored in agreement, the final scoring included thirty-six questions.

In addition to using the questionnaire to code for the presence of positive attributes in the *responses* of the participants, Taylor and colleagues[19] demonstrated that the *questions* in the interview could be related to the model of developmental assets devised by Benson and his colleagues.[20] As such, the set of positive responses in regard to asset categories was placed by two expert independent raters into one of the four internal categories of assets of this model, one of the four external categories of assets of this model, or a demographic category.[21]

The raters agreed on thirty-two of the forty-one interview items (78 percent; Cohen's kappa = .74, $p < .001$). However, six of the items were demographic, and one was not applicable to an asset category. The remaining twenty-five items related to an asset category. No item was placed into the positive identity asset category, and one item ("Do your parents use legal drugs?") was placed into an asset category but the responses to this question could not be scored into positive or not positive. As such, a final set of twenty-four items remained in the pool of "indirectly measured" developmental assets.

Procedure

All interviews were conducted in a setting selected by the youth (a gang or CBO meeting area, a public location such as a restaurant, or the home of the participant or a friend or relative). No attrition occurred across the two waves.

Results

The present analyses were aimed first at interrelating idiographic scores for growth in attributes of positive functioning with scores for individual and ecological developmental assets within and across the two times of measurement completed to date in OTO. Second, we assessed through use of configural frequency analyses[22] whether combinations of positive change trajectories and asset scores characterized the gang or the CBO youth.

Individual (idiographic) analysis of developmental assets and trajectories of positive functioning

As detailed in Chapter Two of this volume, for both the gang and CBO youth the within-participant distribution of positive attribute scores was inspected. Each participant was assigned a score (which could range from zero to 9) for the number of nine attributes whose individual growth curves reflected an increase in positive functioning across the two times of testing. As reported in Chapter Two, these growth scores ranged from 1 to 8 among the gang youth (mean = 5.89, SD = 1.37) and from 6 to 8 among the CBO youth (mean = 6.76, SD = .59).

Each individual's positive functioning "growth" score was correlated with (1) the score he attained for each individual and ecological asset at each time of testing and (2) the change scores for each developmental asset. The results of these analyses are presented in Table 3.1.

As shown in the table, there were few significant correlations between the eight asset scores and growth scores at either time 1 or time 2. For the CBO youth, there was one significant correlation at time 1 and none at time 2. For the gang youth, there were no significant correlations at time 1 and two at time 2. However, the gang and CBO youth differed in regard to the number of significant correlations between growth scores and the difference (change) between time 1 and time 2 asset scores (six and two, respectively; $z = 2.00$, $p < .05$). Therefore, changes over time in positive functioning are linked to developmental assets more so for gang members than for CBO youth.

These analyses therefore indicate assets existing among gang youth and that the assets are associated with their overcoming the

Table 3.1. Correlations between functioning and developmental assets at each time of testing and change scores for developmental assets

	Gang			CBO		
	r Between Growth Score and:			r Between Growth Score and:		
Assets	Time 1	Time 2	T_2-T_1	Time 1	Time 2	T_2-T_1
Support	0.13	0.23	0.52**	0.03	0.16	0.49**
Empowerment	-0.12	0.01	0.21	-0.30*	-0.26	0.17
Boundaries and expectations	-0.07	0.07	0.49**	-0.08	-0.07	0.02
Constructive use of time	0.04	0.37*	0.23	0.04	0.04	0
Commitment to learning	0.04	0.17	0.55**	-0.24	-0.11	0.25
Positive values	-0.03	0.16	0.31*	0.11	0.17	0.11
Social competencies	-0.1	0.47**	0.62**	-0.22	-0.17	0.11
Total asset score	-0.04	0.25	0.67**	-0.13	-0.03	0.57**

Notes: T1 = time 1

T2 = time 2

** Correlation is significant at the 0.01 level (two-tailed)

* Correlation is significant at the 0.05 level (two-tailed)

odds—that is, with positive developmental trajectories. As such, the results summarized in Table 1 suggest that there are individual assets (commitment to learning, positive values, social competencies) and ecological (support, boundaries and expectations) assets that may be important in fostering positive change among gang youth. Accordingly, we sought to ascertain if particular combinations of assets and positive change trajectories were emblematic of gang youth.

Types and antitypes of positive change and assets among the groups

Configural frequency analysis (CFA) methods were developed by von Eye[23] to determine if there are patterns of covariation among categories that occur more often than chance (and form what von Eye calls "types"), and if there are patterns of covariation among categories that occur less often than chance (what von Eye terms "antitypes"). CFAs were used to explore systematically whether there exist specific types of combination of assets and positive growth among the gang youth, and whether these combinations were unique to the sample of OTO gang members or could be identified also among the CBO youth. To address these issues, two sets of six CFAs were computed. The sets were differentiated on the basis of the decision rule used for categorization. In the initial set of six CFAs, categorization was based on a median split, where *high* means at or above the median and *low* is below the median.

The first CFA assessed group (gang, CBO) $\times$ asset change score (high, low) $\times$ positive attribute growth score (high, low). For the gang youth, there was one type (Lehmacher's test, with a continuity correction [L] = 3.03, $p < .05$) and one antitype (L = -2.87, $p < .05$). More gang youth than expected had low asset change scores and low positive attribute growth scores; fewer gang youth than expected had high asset change scores and low positive attribute growth scores. For the CBO youth, there was also one type (L = 3.35, $p < .05$) and one antitype (L = -3.77, $p < .05$). As with the gang youth, more CBO youth than expected had low asset change scores and low positive attribute growth scores; in turn, fewer CBO youth had low asset change scores and high positive attribute growth scores.

The second CFA considered group (gang, CBO) × positive attribute growth score (high, low) × total asset score at time 1 (high, low). There were no types or antitypes found for the gang or the CBO youth. Similarly, the third CFA assessed group (gang, CBO) × attribute growth score (high, low) × total asset score at time 2 (high, low). Again, there were no types or antitypes found for the gang or CBO youth.

The fourth CFA considered group (gang, CBO) × total attribute score at time 2 (high, low) × total asset score at time 2 (high, low). Here, there were two types ($L = 2.88$, $p < .05$; $L = 3.40$, $p < .05$, respectively) and two antitypes ($L = -2.57$, $p < .05$; $L = -3.76$, $p < .05$, respectively) for the gang youth. There were also two types ($L = 4.60$, $p < .05$; $L = 3.08$, $p < .05$, respectively) and two antitypes ($L = -4.23$, $p < .05$; $L = 3.30$, $p < .05$, respectively) for the CBO youth. For both the gang and CBO youth, more individuals than expected had low total attribute scores at time 2 and total low asset scores at time 2. More gang and CBO youth than expected also had high total attribute scores at time 2 and high total asset scores at time 2. Fewer gang and CBO youth than expected had either low total attribute scores at time 2 and high total asset scores at time 2, or high total attribute scores at time 2 and low total asset scores at time 2.

The fifth CFA assessed group (gang, CBO) × total attribute score at time 2 (high, low) × total asset score at time 1 (high, low). There were two types ($L = 3.95$, $p < .05$; $L = 3.31$, $p < .05$, respectively) and two antitypes ($L = -3.80$, $p < .05$; $L = -3.44$, $p < .05$, respectively) for the gang youth. There were also two types ($L = 3.82$, $p < .05$; $L = 3.83$, $p < .05$, respectively) and two antitypes ($L = -3.76$, $p < .05$; $L = -3.88$, $p < .05$, respectively) for the CBO youth. For both the gang and CBO youth, more individuals than expected had low total attribute scores at time 2 and low total asset scores at time 1. More gang and CBO youth than expected also had high total attribute scores at time 2 and high total asset scores at time 1. Fewer gang and CBO youth than expected had either low total attribute scores at time 2 and high total asset scores at time 1, or high total attribute scores at time 2 and low total asset scores at time 1.

Finally, the sixth CFA considered group (gang, CBO) × total attribute score at time 2 (high, low) × total asset change score at time 2 (high, low). There were no types or antitypes found for either gang or CBO youth.

In short, the results of these CFA analyses suggested that there were some situations wherein gang youth did show evidence of overcoming the odds. Specifically, like the CBO youth, gang members had higher scores at time 2 for attributes of positive functioning and had higher asset scores at this time of measurement, as well as at the initial time of testing. In other words, over the one-year time span assessed to date in OTO, developmental assets present at the beginning and the end of this period were related to higher positive functioning at the end of the period among gang youth in a manner similar to that found among CBO youth.

Given that this is exploratory research, we assessed if a different median split rule would result in variation in these findings. Accordingly, we recomputed the six CFAs with categorization based on a median split, where *high* means above the median and *low* means at or below the median. Somewhat different findings were obtained.

The first CFA assessed group (gang, CBO) × asset change score (high, low) × positive attribute growth score (high, low). For the gang youth, there was one type ($L = 2.65, p < .05$) and no antitype. More gang youth than expected had high asset change scores and high positive attribute growth scores. For the CBO youth, there was also one type ($L = 2.56, p < .05$) and no antitype. More CBO youth than expected had low asset change scores and low positive attribute growth scores, and fewer CBO youth had low asset change scores and high positive attribute growth scores.

The second CFA appraised group (gang, CBO) × positive attribute growth score (high, low) × total asset score at time 1 (high, low). There was one type ($L = 3.05, p < .05$) for gang youth and one type for CBO youth ($L = 2.67, p < .05$). More gang youth than expected had high total asset scores at time 1 and high positive attribute growth scores. More CBO youth than expected had low total asset scores at time 1 and low positive attribute growth scores.

The third CFA considered group (gang, CBO) × positive attribute growth score (high, low) × total asset score at time 2 (high, low). There was one type (L = 4.97, $p < .05$) for gang youth and one type for CBO youth (L = 2.67, $p < .05$). More gang youth than expected had high total asset scores at time 2 and high positive attribute growth scores. More CBO youth than expected had low positive attribute growth scores and low total asset scores at time 2.

The fourth CFA assessed group (gang, CBO) × total attribute score at time 2 (high, low) × total asset score at time 2 (high, low). There were two types (L = 3.05, $p < .05$; L = 6.14, $p < .05$, respectively) and two antitypes (L = −3.76, $p < .05$; L = −5.11, $p < .05$, respectively) for the gang youth. There was one type (L = 3.51, $p < .05$) and one antitype (L = −3.66, $p < .05$) for the CBO youth. For both gang and CBO youth, more than expected had low total asset scores at time 2 and low total attribute scores at time 2. Fewer gang and CBO youth than expected had low total asset scores at time 2 and high total attribute scores at time 2. Fewer gang youth than expected had high total asset scores at time 2 and low total attribute scores at time 2.

The fifth CFA considered group (gang, CBO) × total attribute score at time 2 (high, low) × total asset score at time 1 (high, low). There were two types (L = 2.66, $p < .05$; L = 5.69, $p < .05$, respectively) and two antitypes (L = −3.32, $p < .05$; L = −4.71, $p < .05$, respectively) for the gang youth. There were also one type (L = 3.89, $p < .05$) and one antitype (L = −4.09, $p < .05$) for the CBO youth. For both the gang and CBO youth, more individuals than expected had low total attribute scores and high total asset scores at time 1. More gang youth than expected also had high total attribute scores at time 2 and low total asset scores at time 1.

The sixth CFA assessed group (gang, CBO) × total attribute score at time 2 (high, low) × asset change score (high, low). No types or antitypes were found among the gang or CBO youth.

In sum, this second set of CFAs provided some additional evidence of overcoming the odds among gang youth. That is, high levels of assets at times 1 and 2, and high asset change between these two times of testing, were associated among the gang youth with a high level of positive change in attributes of positive functioning. Thus, as in the initial set of CFAs, developmental assets are an important basis for developing positive behaviors among gang youth.

Discussion

The purpose of the Overcoming the Odds project is to test theoretical ideas about the nature of positive youth development within the person-context developmental system.[24] The study is designed to bring longitudinal data to bear on the notion that all young people possess attributes that may be associated with positive development and that such development is furthered by a community setting possessing key assets for healthy growth. We believe that such data may constitute an empirical base for discussion of the programs and policies that should be designed to enhance positive development, especially among those youth stereotypically viewed from the vantage point of a deficit model, one wherein young people are seen as possessing a constellation of problems that require, at best, preventive action aimed at problem management.[25] African American gang youth are prototypically placed in such a deficit category; thus the OTO project seeks to ascertain whether groups of gang youth evince the bases of positive development.

This chapter builds on the findings presented in Chapter Two of this volume to offer more information about whether individual and ecological assets are associated with positive developmental trajectories among the gang and CBO youth. The results indicated that for CBO youth and—in regard to overcoming the odds—for gang youth, growth in attributes of positive functioning were related to scores for individual and ecological developmental assets within and across the two times of measurement and to the change scores for each developmental asset. These findings therefore suggest some individual and ecological assets that are important in fostering positive change among gang youth. These analyses suggest that positive development of gang youth may be sensitive to promotion if adolescents are embedded in an increasingly asset-rich developmental system.

Accordingly, despite the limitations of this research, we believe that one key theoretical implication of our findings is that the lives of gang youth may be enhanced when developmental assets are increasingly interfused within the developmental systems. Such infusion is at the heart of policy recommendations[26] that stress family-centered community building for youth. That is, the lives of all young people can be improved if, at the community level, actions are aimed at increasing the ability of all community members—including young people themselves—to improve the array and integration of the psychosocial "nutrients" needed for healthy behavior and development. Such actions may, as suggested by these analyses, create a subset of gang youth who—despite being embedded in a behavioral and social milieu marked by risks (gang violence, drugs, poor familial support) that transcend the typical problems of poverty and racism—show substantial evidence of positive development. If future research confirms the role of assets in the positive development of gang youth, then there will be increasingly more compelling reasons to proactively support, at a policy level, programs seeking to capitalize on the potential of all young people to have a life marked by behavior contributing to their own healthy behavior and development and that of others.

Notes

1. Taylor, C. S., Lerner, R. M., von Eye, A., Bobek, D., Balsano, A., Dowling, E., & Anderson, P. (in press). Positive individual and social behavior among gang and non-gang African American male adolescents. *Journal of Adolescent Research*. Internal and external developmental assets among African American male gang members. *Journal of Adolescent Research*; Taylor, C. S., Lerner, R. M., von Eye, A., Bobek, D., Bilalbegovic Balsano, A., Dowling, E., & Anderson, P. (in press).

2. Lerner, R. M. (2002). *Concepts and theories of human development* (3rd ed.). Mahwah, NJ: Erlbaum; McAdoo, H. P. (1995). Stress levels, family help patterns, and religiosity in middle- and working-class African American single

mothers. *Journal of Black Psychology, 21,* 424–449; McAdoo, H. P. (1998). African American families: Strength and realities. In H. C. McCubbin, E. Thompson, & J. Futrell (Eds.), *Resiliency in ethnic minority families: African American families* (pp. 17–30). Thousand Oaks, CA: Sage; McAdoo, H. P. (1999). Diverse children of color. In H. E. Fitzgerald, B. M. Lester, & B. S. Zuckerman (Eds.), *Children of color: Research, health, and policy issues* (pp. 205–218). New York: Garland; Spencer, M. B. (1990). Development of minority children: An introduction. *Child Development, 61,* 267–269; Spencer, M. B. (1995). Old issues and new theorizing about African American youth: A phenomenological variant of ecological systems theory. In R. L. Taylor (Ed.), *Black youth: Perspectives on their status in the United States* (pp. 38–69). Westport, CT: Praeger; Spencer, M. B. (1999). Social and cultural influences on school adjustment: The application of an identity-focused cultural ecological perspective. *Educational Psychologist, 34,* 43–57; Spencer, M. B., Harpalani, V., Fegley, S., Dell'Angelo, T., & Seaton, G. (in press). Identity, self, and peers in context: A culturally-sensitive, developmental framework for analysis. In R. M. Lerner, F. Jacobs, & D. Wertlieb (Eds.), *Applying developmental science for youth and families: Historical and theoretical foundations: Vol. 1. Handbook of applied developmental science: Promoting positive child, adolescent, and family development through research, policies, and programs.* Thousand Oaks, CA: Sage; Spencer, M. B., Dupress, D., & Hartmann, T. (1997). A phenomenological variant of ecological systems theory (PVEST): A self-organization perspective in context. *Development and Psychopathology, 9,* 817–833.

3. Spencer (1995); Spencer, Dupress, & Hartmann (1997).

4. Spencer (1990).

5. Benson, P. (1997). *All kids are our kids: What communities must do to raise caring and responsible children and adolescents.* San Francisco: Jossey-Bass; Benson, P. (in press a). Building communities for healthy youth and families: A vision for the future. In R. M. Lerner & P. Benson (Eds.), *Developmental assets and asset-building communities: Implications for research, policy, and programs.* Norwell, MA: Kluwer; Benson, P. (in press b). Developmental assets and asset-building communities: Implications for research, policy, and practice. In Lerner & Benson; Benson, P. L., & Pittman, K. J. (Eds.). (2001). *Trends in youth development: Visions, realities, and challenges.* Norwell, MA: Kluwer.

6. Dryfoos, J. G. (1990). *Adolescents at risk: Prevalence and prevention.* New York: Oxford University Press; Huston, A. C. (1991). *Children in poverty: Child development and public policy.* Cambridge: Cambridge University Press.

7. Taylor et al. (in press a); Taylor et al. (in press b).

8. McAdoo (1995); McAdoo (1998); McAdoo (1999); Luster, T., & McAdoo, H. P. (1994). Factors related to the achievement and adjustment of young African American children. *Child Development, 65,* 1080–1094; Luster, T., & McAdoo, H. (1996). Family and child influences on educational attainment: A secondary analysis of the High/Scope Perry Preschool data. *Developmental Psychology, 32*(1), 26–39.

9. Spencer (1990); Spencer (1995); Spencer (1999); Spencer, Dupress, & Hartmann (1997).

10. Benson (1997); Benson (in press a); Benson (in press b); Benson and Pittman (2001).

11. Taylor, C. S. (1990). *Dangerous society*. East Lansing: Michigan State University Press; Taylor, C. S. (1993). *Girls, gangs, women, and drugs*. East Lansing: Michigan State University Press; Taylor, C. S. (1996, January). The unintended consequences of incarceration: Youth development, the juvenile corrections systems, and crime. Paper presented at the Vera Institute Conference, Harriman, NY; Taylor, C. S. (2001). Youth gangs. In N. J. Smelser & P. B. Baltes (Eds.), *International encyclopedia of the social and behavioral sciences* (pp. 16664–16668). Oxford: Elsevier.

12. Taylor, C. S., Lerner, R. M., von Eye, A., Balsano, A. B., Dowling, E. M., Anderson, P. M., Bobek, D. L., & Bjelobrk, D. (in press). Stability of attributes of positive functioning and of developmental assets among African American adolescent male gang and community-based organization youth.

13. Thelen, E., & Smith, L. B. (1998). Dynamic systems theories. In W. Damon (Series Ed.) & R. M. Lerner (Vol. Ed.), *Handbook of child psychology: Vol. 1. Theoretical models of human development* (5th ed., pp. 563–633). New York: Wiley.

14. Gore, A. (in press). Foreword. In Lerner & Benson; Gore, A. & Gore, T. (in press). *Joined at the Heart: The Transformation of the American Family*. New York: Holt.

15. von Eye, A. (Ed.) (1990a). *Statistical methods in longitudinal research: Vol.1. Principles and structuring change*. New York: Academic Press; von Eye, A. (Ed.) (1990b). *Statistical methods in longitudinal research: Vol.2. Time series and categorical longitudinal data*. New York: Academic Press; von Eye, A. (2002). *Configural frequency analysis: Methods, models, applications*. Mahwah, NJ: Erlbaum.

16. Taylor et al. (in press a); Taylor et al. (in press b); and Chapter Two of this volume.

17. Taylor (1990); Taylor (1993); Taylor (1996); Taylor (2001).

18. Taylor et al. (in press b).

19. Taylor et al. (in press a).

20. Benson (1997); Benson, P. L., Leffert, N., Scales, P. C., & Blyth, D. A. (1998). Beyond the "village" rhetoric: Creating healthy communities for children and adolescents. *Applied Developmental Science, 2*(3), 138–159.

21. These raters were Peter Scales and Nancy Leffert, key colleagues in the developmental asset work of Search Institute. See also Leffert, N., Benson, P. L., Scales, P. C., Sharma, A. R., Drake, D. R., & Blyth, D. A. (1998). Developmental assets: Measurement and predication of risk behaviors among adolescents. *Applied Developmental Science, 2*, 209–230; Scales, P. C., & Leffert, N. (1999). *Developmental assets: A synthesis of the scientific research on adolescent development*. Minneapolis: Search Institute; Scales, P. C., Benson, P. L., Leffert, N., & Blyth, D. A. (2000). Contribution of developmental assets to the prediction of thriving among adolescents. *Applied Developmental Science, 4*(1), 27–46.

22. Von Eye (1990a); von Eye (1990b); von Eye (2002).

23. Von Eye (1990a); von Eye (1990b); von Eye (2002).

24. Benson (1997); Benson (in press a); Benson (in press b); Lerner (2002).

25. Roth, J., Brooks-Gunn, J., Murray, L., & Foster, W. (1998). Promoting healthy adolescents: Synthesis of youth development program evaluations. *Journal of Research on Adolescence, 8,* 423–459.

26. Benson (in press a); Gore (in press); Gore & Gore (in press).

CARL S. TAYLOR *is professor in the Department of Family and Child Ecology at Michigan State University.*

RICHARD M. LERNER *is the Bergstrom Chair in Applied Developmental Science in the Eliot-Pearson Department of Child Development at Tufts University.*

ALEXANDER VON EYE *is professor in the Department of Psychology at Michigan State University.*

AIDA BILALBEGOVIC BALSANO, ELIZABETH M. DOWLING, *and* PAMELA M. ANDERSON *are doctoral students in the Eliot-Pearson Department of Child Development at Tufts University.*

DEBORAH L. BOBEK *is managing director of the Applied Developmental Science Institute at Tufts University.*

DRAGANA BJELOBRK *is a doctoral student in the Department of Family and Child Ecology at Michigan State University.*

This chapter presents Spencer's phenomenological variant of ecological systems theory, or PVEST (1995), as a conceptual framework for examining positive youth development. Contextual factors affecting racial and gender identity of African American youth are discussed, with the focus on the influence of schools and religious institutions.

4

Identity processes and the positive youth development of African Americans: An explanatory framework

*Dena Phillips Swanson, Margaret Beale Spencer,
Tabitha Dell'Angelo, Vinay Harpalani,
Tirzah R. Spencer*

A CENTRAL TASK for researchers who seek to facilitate positive youth development is to fully understand the multifaceted, eco-culturally linked character of human development. This requires understanding how social, political, cultural, and historical contexts interact with and influence identity formation. Identity lays the foundation for how youths view themselves and their future prospects. To understand these interactive and complex processes and to increase positive and resilient outcomes among youth, it is

Note: Preparation of this manuscript was supported in part by grants from the National Institutes of Mental Health, the National Science Foundation, the Kellogg Foundation, and the Ford Foundation awarded to the second author.

critical to analyze and comprehend relationships between the environments they encounter, acknowledge their perceptions and reactions to these environments, and assess their consequent maturational and developmental trajectories. Accordingly, a listing of their assets and liabilities alone is not adequate. Instead, a multifaceted approach, incorporating identity, culture, and context while emphasizing developmental processes, is warranted.

In this paper, we describe Spencer's[1] phenomenological variant of ecological systems theory (PVEST) as a conceptual framework that embodies such an approach. Although PVEST is a general life-course theory of human development applicable across groups, we focus our attention here on African American youth. Myriad conceptual flaws and misunderstandings characterize scholarship on black youth: deficit-oriented assumptions, lack of developmental perspective, inappropriate avoidance of racial and ethnic themes, and the absence of a normative and comprehensive theoretical framework. We view PVEST as a corrective to these flaws and present the conceptual frame and its applications to illustrate its broad utility.

Identity is an extremely complex construction that has multiple domains. However, it is impossible to cover the full range of identity domains in this chapter. We lay out general concepts central to identity formation, such as self-appraisal, and focus largely on the interaction of racial and gender identity for black youth. We also acknowledge that development occurs across multiple contexts, but we focus on schools and religious institutions. These are presented as contexts where identity formation and related developmental processes occur for African American youth. Our aim is to illustrate that theory-driven formulations that are sensitive to the complex and dynamic nature of human development are necessary to understand and promote positive youth development.

Identity processes

Identity can be viewed as the central psychological element that defines and maintains an individual's sense of self and "other" through developmental changes. In the course of engaging "normative" stress while transitioning across social settings and coping with these encounters, identity processes become defined specifically by how individuals make meaning of their own experiences and the contexts they encounter at multiple levels. Multiple selves emerge and are defined as this occurs. Our theoretical framework, Spencer's PVEST,[2] integrates identity and self-appraisal process with experiences in contexts and subsequent life outcomes. Unavoidable self-appraisal processes, which involve evaluating one's own standing with regard to one's bidirectional experiences in multiple contexts, are crucial in identity development. As part of the life course of African Americans, identity involves appraising or assessing one's social status as a minority group member and making meaning of this social information. Particularly for African American youth, experience varies by gender in response to stereotypic assumptions about race, masculinity, and femininity, and the interactions between these race and gender stereotypes. Thus, given the prevalence of gender-linked racial stereotypes, an informed consideration of African American youth development must entail understanding not just what it means to be black but what it means to be a black American male or female as a story of assets and liabilities.

The phenomenological variant of ecological systems theory (PVEST)

PVEST[3] builds a bridge between identity and context, although the latter is "tinted" by the nature of race and ethnicity and gender-linked stereotypes. By applying a phenomenological perspective to Bronfenbrenner's ecological systems theory,[4] PVEST allows us to analyze self-appraisal and meaning-making processes, as a dynamic system, within the various contexts of development (school, family, neighborhood). These processes, evolving over time, maturation, and space, underlie identity development and life outcomes.[5] PVEST offers a framework to examine normative human development, through the interaction of identity and context character. It takes into account individual and group-level differences in experience, perception, and negotiation of stress and dissonance (or lack thereof). As such, PVEST uses an *identity-focused cultural-ecological* perspective, integrating issues of social, historical, and cultural context with normative maturational and developmental processes that youth undergo.[6]

PVEST is conceptualized as five basic components linked by bidirectional, recursive processes, forming a dynamic, cyclic model (see Figure 4.1). The first component, *net vulnerability level*, essentially consists of the contexts and characteristics that can potentially pose a challenge during an individual's development at any life stage. A risk contributor is a factor that may predispose the individual for adverse outcomes during a particular developmental stage. Risk contributors function as a liability that, of course, may be offset by corresponding stage-specific protective factors (such as cultural capital). For marginalized youth (those of color and low-resource youth), risk includes such socioeconomic conditions as poverty, imposed expectations regarding race and gender stereotypes, and larger historical processes

Figure 4.1. A phenomenological variant of ecological systems theory, or PVEST

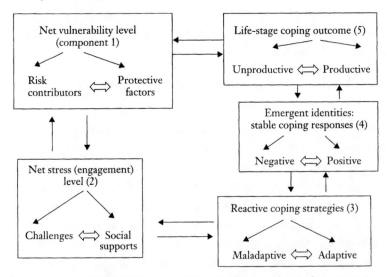

Source: Spencer, M. B. "Old Issues and New Theorizing About African American Youth: A Phenomenological Variant of Ecological Systems Theory." In R. L. Taylor (ed.), *Black Youth: Perspectives on Their Status in the United States.* Westport, Conn.: Praeger, 1995.

including racial subordination and discrimination. Risk and protective factors, filtered through multiple levels of context (macrosystem, mesosystem, microsystem)[7] are unavoidably and bidirectionally linked because too much of one without a corresponding balance of the other affects net vulnerability. Self-appraisal is a key factor in identity formation; perception of the risks one faces and the protective resources available are central to identity processes and development.

Net stress engagement level, the second component of PVEST, refers to the actual experience of a situation challenging an individual's well-being; this is risk that is actually encountered and juxtaposed against available support. Available social support can help a young person negotiate an experience of stress; thus, a support is an actualized protective factor. Virtually unconscious equilibrating efforts, which also affect future vulnerability, occur as the individual engages these stresses and supports. Experience of racism—both subtle and overt—and related dissonance are salient stressors for youth of color. These experiences compound the normative developmental issues that all adolescents must confront (puberty, identity exploration, peer relationships). One's history of cultural socialization can serve as a protective factor in this process, and available adult role models can be supports to help a youth reactively cope with these experiences.

In response to stressors and in conjunction with supports, *reactive coping methods* are employed to resolve a dissonance-producing situation. Normative cognitive maturation makes awareness of dissonance acute and unavoidable. Reactive coping responses include problem-solving strategies that a youth employs to deal with stress and dissonance. These can lead to either an adaptive or a maladaptive solution; as noted by Howard Stevenson,[8] a solution can be adaptive in one context (such as neighborhood) and maladaptive in another (school).

As a youth employs various coping strategies, self-appraisal continues; those strategies that produce desirable results for the ego, whether adaptive or maladaptive, are, with redundant usage, replicated. Accordingly, these become stable coping responses; coupled together, they yield emergent patterned responses or identities.

Emergent identities define how individuals view themselves within and between their various contexts of development (family, school, neighborhood) and may show stability over time as well as space. The combination of cultural and ethnic identity, sex role understanding, and self and peer appraisal all help to define one's identity.

Identity lays the foundation for future perception, self-appraisal, and behavior, yielding adverse or productive *life-stage, specific coping outcomes*. Productive outcomes include good health, positive relationships, and high self-esteem, while adverse outcomes include poor health, incarceration, and self-destructive behavior.

The PVEST framework represents dynamic processes that continue throughout the life span as individuals encounter and balance new risks against protective factors, engage new stressors (potentially offset by supports), establish more expansive coping strategies, and redefine how they view themselves, which also affects how others view them. As noted by Erikson,[9] unresolved issues within one life stage influence future coping and identity formation processes. An ICE (identity-focused cultural-ecological) perspective specifies the nature and character of intervening processes. PVEST aims not only to capture this entire developmental process but also to place it within its broader social contexts.

Self-appraisal

The self-appraisal processes integrate various aspects of one's life that promote development of a strong sense of personal identity and represent cognitive, affective, and social undergirding processes. As perceptions of the self are gained through interaction with the environment, ethnic and racial identity represents an integral aspect of minority youth development and life course competence formation. Cultural values are an important aspect of accrued knowledge because they afford the adolescent information necessary to interpret and proactively respond to environmental experiences and stereotypical messages concerning minority status.[10]

Developing a sense of efficacy is crucial during adolescence because of the youth's heightened self-consciousness and increasing cognitive awareness. Development, however, is partially determined by the opportunities, limitations, and expectations that society makes available to the individual. Successful performance on a particular task increases a sense of personal empowerment (that is, competence) and the likelihood of future success in subsequent tasks. Given the general developmental tasks associated with early adolescence, issues of competence are compounded by one's culture as well as one's status in the larger society. Therefore, competence is rooted in culture and prior successes, and it appears crucial for successful adaptation to subsequent adult roles.

As described by Spencer and Dupree[11] and suggested by Bandura's theorizing,[12] self-system development is reciprocally determined from self-other appraisal processes. Particularly during middle childhood, these recursive self-other evaluative processes appear to be unavoidably linked to the experience of stress. The stress response requires coping, which leads to stable psychosocial responses that may be maladaptive or adaptive. Stable psychosocial coping strategies are linked to a coping outcome or product that may be either productive in quality (competency, self-efficacy, resiliency) or unproductive (school avoidance, acting-out behavior, leaving school, dropping out). These coping outcomes set the stage for the recursive and subsequent experience of context, given individual self-other appraisal processes, as the individual progresses developmentally over the life course.

There are several unique characteristics of individual coping strategies among adolescents. Relevant aspects of cognitive and social development include self-perception, self-efficacy, self-esteem, intelligence, temperament, and problem-solving and interpersonal skills.[13] Individual attributes develop as a function of behaviors or beliefs that reflect an active, selective, structuring orientation toward the environment. The ability to modify, select, and reconstruct the environment, however, depends on one's being enabled or empowered to engage in behavior that influences the environment. The environmental context (or social structures and conditions, from micro- to macro-level systems) offers relevant experiences that interact with psychological processes to produce unique behavior. In sum, the individual is engaged in a life-course process of coping with environmental challenges (risk and stress), sociocultural contexts (expectations, attitudes, cultural beliefs and assumptions), and normative developmental tasks.[14]

Gender identity

When examined over time, parents are often viewed as providing different socialization experiences for males and females. Significant attention has been given to analyzing father absence and female-headed households and subsequent identity processes. Males are often encouraged to be physical and allowed significant independence, while females are frequently assisted rather than encouraged toward independence and mastery. Although men tend to encourage more gender-associated activities in their children, both parents tend to be generally attentive and controlling toward same-sex children. The latter finding indicates that males and females may present differential outcomes to father absence versus mother absence.[15] To illustrate, it has been suggested that boys who are reared in a female-headed home without a positive male figure often lack adequate identification with a male role model. Accordingly, these youngsters may overcompensate for a sense of masculinity by demonstrating excessively aggressive, assertive, and often antisocial behavior patterns.[16] This tendency may have disastrous implications for educational experiences, which most often occur in a female-predominant learning environment where women represent the source of directives for academic performance and behavioral expectations.[17]

Harris, Gold, and Henderson's study[18] examined the influence of father absence on gender-role orientation and achievement for a sample of older African American and white female adolescents. Although prior findings indicate that fathers play an important role in forming traditional traits in daughters, Harris and colleagues expected females without fathers to exhibit greater masculine-linked attributes and have higher achievement motives. Their findings indicated that for their African American girls (although not supported for the overall sample), data patterns indicated significantly higher achievement needs and higher masculinity and androgynous attributes. The extent to which this finding reflects a characteristic of female-headed (father absence) outcomes or represents part of the cultural socialization experience associated with the multiple roles of African American females is a critical consideration. Ladner's research[19] on sex role development indicates that positive characteristics of adulthood, including strength and independence, are less sex-role differentiated among poor African American adolescents than among their European American, middle-class counterparts. Ladner suggests that multiple gender roles have been a reality for African American women for generations. Their identity, defined in terms of additional roles other than mother and wife, stands in contrast to white middle-class American women for whom dual roles are a more recent phenomenon. There may be important implications for competing male adolescent youths' masculinity needs.

As reported by Swanson and Spencer,[20] traditional masculinity as experienced in Western societies includes engaging in certain behaviors that are not socially sanctioned but that nevertheless validate masculinity. Male adolescents may perceive themselves as masculine, and in fact believe that others also share this perception, if they engage in risk-taking behaviors such as premarital sex, alcohol and drugs, and delinquent activities. For African American male youth who feel frequently challenged because they face myriad expressions of structural racism, risk-taking behavioral patterns may be viewed as salient for guaranteeing their view of self as a man. It is not surprising, then, that girls and boys perceive a neighborhood police presence as having quite contrasting meanings and serving different potential sources of stress and self-definition.[21]

Although often anecdotally reported, African American parents describe the additional developmental task of having to instruct their male children on how to respond to police officers so as to ensure that behavior is not misconstrued as threatening or aggressive. This child-rearing strategy reduces the probability of their black son becoming a victim of police brutality at worst or simple harassment at best.[22] Thus, for minority parents, child-rearing efforts require clear explanation of minority status and its meaning and significance relative to race, gender, body type, physical size, and response to authority.

American culture and the minority experience are themes explained by some parents to their sons as cultural socialization. However, such explicit socialization is not typically the norm, although its protective function in support of positive youth development has been established.[23] Still, the differential experiences of black males and the related stress remain present even when not made explicit. In the context of such a culture, youth having similar experiences can exhibit either resiliency and school adjustment or problem behavior and academic disengagement. Unfortunately, the complexities of these processes are not well understood for youth who chronically struggle with difficult conditions. Too frequently, they are stereotyped as lacking appropriate moral fabric.[24]

According to gender intensification hypothesis,[25] observed sex differences between adolescent males and females are largely due to accelerated gender-based expectations resulting in stereotypic masculine and feminine behavior. The "intensification" is a particular manifestation of the youth's need to be accepted in his or her expanding social groups as an early step toward developing behavioral autonomy. More often than not, particularly for minorities and low-resource youngsters, given the problem of stigmatization, racism, and socioeconomic inequity, youth often infer a lack of respect frequently accorded others. Their efforts toward acceptability, and development of the greater independence expected of developing adolescents, are often confounded by their experience within the broader society frequently reflecting a hostile context or minimally supportive environment. Demanding and demonstrating independence and responsibility occur early and are recognized in particular microsystems such as family, school, and church. Many low-resource minority youth find themselves moving into a position that demands responsible and independent behavior, but they lack the necessary support.

For example, many black males believe that their behavior is misinterpreted and their academic efforts not respected by the school system. African American males are perhaps the most highly stigmatized and stereotyped group in American society. This creates a context of enormous risk with regard to positive youth development. If respect from the broader society, and particularly the school setting, is not generally forthcoming, gender-intensified behavior such as hypermasculinity may be seen by the youth as potentially more effective in generating respect; in fact, it may add to group stigma and further undermine school adjustment. Thus, from a PVEST perspective, the presence of proper supports, such as cultural socialization efforts and parental monitoring,[26] can lead to adaptive coping and promote positive identity formation, eventually resulting in positive youth development.

Compared to males, adolescent females are documented as experiencing greater emotional barriers, anxiety, and regressive reaction, when confronting a problem-solving situation.[27] Adolescents who generally demonstrate high self-confidence also show high heuristic competence, good social cognitive ability, and an active or proactive adaptation to stress. All of these are assets for positive youth development. Generally, association of stress exposure (for example, to school-based competence) shows that a youth with limited family support and low perceived competence is also likely to be disruptive when experiencing a high level of stress.[28] Males appear less socially competent than females and, when stress is high, appear to be less protected by positive family supports. These variations by gender, as well as the difference in stress reactivity, can inform interventions designed to promote resilience.

Gender-typed characteristics, specifically a female's level of masculinity, reflect a sense of efficacy and control that has been linked to depressive symptomatology. Females with few masculinity attributes score higher on measures of depression than their female counterparts with a high level of masculinity. There is a need to actively assist adolescent females in translating their positive academic experiences into positive youth outcomes and life-course attributes. This is particularly relevant when considering that multiple gender roles have been a reality for African American women for generations, with less sex-role differentiation among them than among their Anglo counterparts. This trend is not expected to drastically change in the near future, and adolescent females need preparation and support to successfully negotiate the anticipated roles.

It is assumed that because females do not exhibit behavioral problems to the same extent or magnitude as males they are experiencing a successful transition into adulthood, barring such social problems as pregnancy or drug abuse. Although adolescent females fare better than males generally, there remains the need for active assistance in translating positive attributes during the transition to adulthood into broad life-course opportunities. As long as females feel positive about their school experience and are demonstrating responsible behavior at home, they appear to possess the attributes necessary for pursuing life goals.[29] The potential concern, however, is whether certain attitudes and behaviors "mask" stressful experiences and whether these attitudes are maladaptive toward later life-course opportunities and experience for females. Hill and her colleagues[30] found that multiple stressful life events increase the vulnerability of children to adverse social and emotional outcomes, and that certain intervening variables such as social support act to protect some children from the impact of these stressors, thus leading to competence and resiliency.

Additionally, another issue of pertinence to African American youth, with regard to stress reactivity and health, is obesity. Gender is also central in this realm. In examining gender differences in stress-induced eating, Grunberg and Straub[31] found that under conditions of emotionally induced stress, there was decreased food consumption among males while females' consumption increased. Stressed women additionally ate twice as much sweet food as unstressed women. Another study compared the amount of food eaten, as self-reported by girls and boys, on the day of an exam (stress) compared to food eaten on a day when no exam was taken. Only girls indicated a significant increase in amount of food (high in fat) eaten on the day of the exam.[32] Previous studies have also examined the impact that emotion-induced eating in children has on intake of sugar and fat. Such studies suggest that the relationship is stronger for African American girls than for European American girls.[33] From a PVEST perspective, this difference may be attributable to coping strategies employed in response to a stressful life event. Thus, pathways to resilience, in terms of health and well-being (both physical and psychological), may vary with the coping strategies.

A related developmental issue that must be considered for girls (and also for boys, although not as well studied) is body image. Research findings have suggested differences in body image perceptions between black and white adolescent girls. For example, Parker and colleagues[34] found that black adolescent females typically do not aspire to an "ideal" body image. Rather, they tend to emphasize those individually desirable features that they already have. In contrast, many white adolescent females do aspire to a societal ideal: the so-called Barbie doll image. These contrasting concepts of body image have implications for gender identity. This example also illustrates how proactive cultural socialization can promote positive youth development; it may serve as a buffer against the stresses that adolescent girls face regarding beauty ideals.

Contexts of development

As we have noted, identity formation cannot be studied in a vacuum; this has been the error of much psychological research. The interaction of developmental processes and contextualized experiences, along with the meaning that youth apply to these experiences, is necessary for any salient understanding of human development. For African American youth, experiences of racism characterize many of the spaces encountered in everyday life; however, other spaces can serve as supports. School experiences and religious institutions represent salient contexts of development for black youth.

School experiences

As a mechanism for instilling competence, academic success during adolescence is a significant factor in determining life-course choices. School is an environment critical to the psychosocial development of adolescents. Students' academic experiences can either support or undermine normative developmental processes. Individuals develop and adapt through interactions that occur within a particular environmental setting.[35] Academic achievement and positive school experiences are therefore essential during early and middle adolescence in facilitating healthy identity development and a sense of competence.

According to Erikson,[36] developing a sense of efficacy (industry versus inferiority) requires initiating and managing aspects of the environment that are significant. This process may be enhanced by positive identification with a competent adult. However, if the possibility of success proves elusive and social encouragement too weak, a sense of inadequacy and inferiority may be fostered,[37] potentially impeding academic accomplishment and thus future job marketability. During adolescence, student role conflict can seriously impede personal competence, generate aimlessness, and erode social commitment.[38] Therefore, adaptive coping within the academic setting becomes critical for facilitating competence.

Minority status itself represents an aspect of the self that offers a framework for defining parameters for life-course choices and opportunities. Students who hold low evaluation of their academic competence and general self-worth usually perform poorly in school, lose interest in academic activities, and are likely to be truant. This disengagement is exhibited not only in truancy but also in a low level of participation in school activities and delinquency in the form of school violence and vandalism.[39]

Wide variations exist in school experience, particularly in relation to environmental risk, resource availability, family relations, and job-training opportunities for poor African American youth. These ecologically nested experiences have implications for any identity formation process. The psychosocial implications of academic competence are a pivotal resource for healthy and positive identity development during adolescence, and also for navigating the difficult transition to gainful employment in adulthood. Too often, public school policies and practices frustrate the minority student's effort to prepare educationally for a successful school-to-work transition into adulthood. Systematic school-linked barriers facing minority youth, particularly males, result in repeated academic failure and discouragement regarding future occupational prospects.[40] Jencks and Meyers[41] reported that adolescents who are reared in an affluent neighborhood obtain more years of schooling than those from a similar family structure in a poorer neighborhood. These factors influence psychological processes that ascertain whether a student pursues achievement goals, establish which goals are pursued, and determine how effectively the aspirations are pursued.

Expressing vulnerable attitudes (negativity) during adolescence is counterproductive to competent functioning. Negative learning attitudes affect willingness to engage in academic activity, while aggressive and inhibitive attitudes affect expression of externalizing and internalizing behaviors, respectively. These are linked to perception of positive and negative contextual experiences that either support or impede their expression. In the classroom, another risk factor for the student is how the teacher perceives ability on the basis of variables such as gender or ethnicity. Perceived negative teacher expectations and low ego resilience were previously found to consistently predict negative learning and aggressive attitudes among males.[42] For males, these vulnerable attitudes reflect a way of concealing inadequacies accompanied by perceived negative expectations.

Bennett and Bennett[43] found that 55 percent of female teachers and 34 percent of male teachers believe female students will be more successful in all academic areas. Their study concluded that teachers attribute different causation of success and failure on the basis of their own belief system. In essence, the education that male and female students receive depends upon how the teacher perceives and reacts to the student's performance. Other studies concentrate on the possibility that race and the teacher's perception of physical attractiveness play a role in expectations of student's ability.

Marwit[44] investigated the claim that teachers judged the behavior of black students more severely than that of white students. In Marwit's study, the researcher showed teachers a fabricated "incident report," professionally lettered to appear to be from a school in Washington, D.C. In the study, the report described either throwing a tantrum in class or stealing lunch money from a teacher's desk. In the upper-right corner was a picture of a ten-year-old boy, either white or black. Attached to the report was a list of fifteen statements regarding the severity of the incident, recommended disciplinary action, or character evaluation. The results of this study were that teachers' ratings of a black child's transgression were significantly more severe than those of a white child.

Along the same lines, DeMeis and Turner[45] designed a study to assess the effects of a student's race and dialect on teacher evaluation of the student. This study found that student evaluations are affected by variables such as race and dialect. In addition, student performance was highly correlated with teacher rating. The correlation between teacher rating and student performance could be due to the teacher's expert ability and experience with students, or it could be that once the teacher decides what the student is capable of, that is all the teacher expects from the student. The fact that teacher ratings were affected by race and dialect suggests those teachers may have lower expectations of some students. The problem with low expectations is that if the teacher expects the students to perform only at a mediocre level, he or she is less likely to try new methods or offer extra encouragement to a low-expectancy student. Conversely, if a student is expected to do well and is not performing, the teacher is more likely to search for the problem and attempt to remedy it.

Low expectations from teachers can be manifested in numerous ways. A subtle facet of racial stereotyping in schools that can create stress for African American youth is lenient feedback from teachers. Harber[46] describes an empirical study demonstrating that white undergraduates were more likely to provide lenient feedback on the content of a written essay to black students than to white students. Although more research is needed to determine the consequences of this phenomenon, other studies have pointed to distrust of positive feedback. One study noted by Harber[47] actually indicated that black students may become so wary of false praise from whites that receiving it may cause their self-esteem to drop; moreover, this effect occurred only when the black participant was aware of the race of the evaluator. Thus, how black students cope with feedback from teachers also has important implications. This work also illustrates how a seemingly positive action can have unintended harmful results. Thus, in promoting positive youth development for black youth, one must be wary of superficial reinforcements that do not have a substantive basis, particularly with regard to academic matters.

Having expectations about students is not abnormal or necessarily harmful, but unwillingness to modify expectations can be detrimental. If teachers are willing to accept that their initial assessment of a student is wrong and allow flexibility in expectations, this might be acceptable. However, research indicates that teachers seem very confident in their ability to predict the future success of their students. Even worse, the criteria the teachers use for prediction are quite dubious. Adams and Cohen[48] found that teachers in their study believed family background is the best predictor of school success. In addition, the teacher's knowledge of the students' communication (verbal) abilities did not affect predictions made on the basis of social behavior and family background.

Even though there are many limitations to receiving effective education in schools—funding, home situation, other external circumstances—there are factors that teachers can affect. Whether the effect is positive or negative is an important question. Research has suggested a clear relationship between the teacher's expectations of an individual student and a child's subsequent academic performance[49]; also, findings indicate that teachers make judgments about a child's academic performance on the basis of a variety of nonacademic factors: name, gender, physical characteristics, ethnic background, socioeconomic status, and the like.[50] Teachers' beliefs about their students may be communicated in direct classroom interaction or nonverbally. The issue is whether or not the students perceive this differential treatment and translate it into self-evaluation about their own ability.

Brophy[51] focused much attention on how teachers form negative views and whether or not their opinions can be changed. The fact that certain children of particular ethnic, gender, and socioeconomic groups are disproportionately the target of negative teacher expectancies is of great concern.[52] Cooper and Good[53] hypothesize that teachers try to keep control over their classroom interactions by discouraging participation from the less predictable and controllable low achievers.

As a systems theory with an identity-focused cultural-ecological (ICE) perspective, the PVEST framework can help conceptualize how teachers' perceptions of their students become a form of stress engagement for the students and why a predisposition for depression is a risk factor for this stress engagement. As noted, when youth process the information they experience, it influences how they give meaning to aspects of themselves.[54] Feedback from teachers and other significant adults is an important source of feedback and self-appraisal. Such feedback can promote adaptive or maladaptive coping strategies with regard to school and help to shape the student's identity processes and school engagement.

For African American youth, the relationship between racial identity and academic achievement has often been viewed as oppositional with regard to cultural values.[55] However, such assumptions of cultural pathology are not valid; identification with school achievement is a function of identity processes, mediated by self-appraisal and feedback from various sources in the school context. Far from being culturally devalued, educational attainment continues to be regarded as a means of obtaining a secure future for many African American youth. Prior research has supported the role of racial identity as facilitating this process. In particular, studies have shown that youth who subscribe to a Eurocentric, or outgroup, orientation perform less well academically than their peers with a positive black identity.[56] Such an orientation is more compromising to one's mental health and school performance than a positive own-group or inclusionary orientation. This is further evidence for the role of cultural socialization in promoting positive youth development.

Many minority adolescents exhibiting problem behaviors are also likely to be among those with the fewest economic resources and inadequate educational experiences. The significance of self-appraisal processes, church support that encourages spirituality, and school experiences that foster competence is underscored as factors contributing to positive development among African American youth. An understanding of identity processes is critical for interpreting both aversive and advantageous life-course experiences. Other contributing factors not explicitly discussed are educational aspirations, level of ego development, parental and "other kin" support, and cognitive maturity.

Religious institutions and involvement

Conceptualized as a multifaceted resource and protective factor, spirituality and religious engagement has gained increased visibility and scholarly attention with regard to promoting resilience. As a time of identity formation, adolescence encompasses examination of one's attributes and qualities in anticipation of adult roles in family, work, and society. This process incorporates examination of one's values, both cultural and spiritual, in solidifying a belief system.[57] As noted earlier, cultural values that are embedded in ethnic and racial identity give youth the knowledge to respond to environmental experiences and stereotypical messages.[58] These same values also apply to the role of spirituality.

Spirituality and racial identity reflect cognitive structuring that changes in response to the individual's maturational level *and* interactions within his or her environment.[59] Adolescents often question and address contradiction they note in their experience and observation. Characteristic of this period, young people are interpreting with greater scrutiny the inconsistencies that exist in the lives of people around them, across the country, and around the globe. They began examining what Chestang[60] refers to as societal inconsistency, a discrepancy between what society proposes to support and what is actually done. The developmental issues faced during adolescence and the enhanced cognitive processes are a natural transition from what Fowler[61] theorizes as conventional to postconventional faith: youth are expected to move from a spiritual orientation that is extrinsic in nature to one reflecting greater personal commitment and greater investment associated with an intrinsic orientation.

Undergirding the experiences of risk are self-appraisal processes that constitute an interpretational or cognitive frame for assessing and coping with life experiences. Multiple challenges in the youth's environment increase the likelihood of encountering negative situations. The continual demand to respond to situational stressors and pursue less threatening contexts becomes a defining factor in the pattern of stable psychosocial processes. Negative experiences require energy to buffer and effectively cope, allowing less energy for productive development of identity leading to healthy, productive life-course outcomes. Expressing vulnerable attitudes (negativity, hypermasculinity) in response to a challenging context undermines positive approaches toward normative developmental tasks and becomes counterproductive to exploration and competent functioning, thus potentially impeding positive youth development and outcomes.

Adolescent participation in productive activities is critical for buffering the effects of negative contextual experiences and enhancing emotional well-being, irrespective of race.[62] Much of the focus on the role of religiosity has addressed mental health issues relevant to adolescence.[63] Particular attention is given to problem behaviors such as drug abuse[64] and delinquency.[65] Although addressing violence prevention, Meyer and Lausell[66] argue for understanding the adolescent's development and belief system.

It is important to consider the impact of a youth's religious involvement not only in terms of mental health concerns but also in the broader context such as school and community. Trusty and Watts,[67] using a national sample of high school seniors, found frequent religious activity and positive religious attitudes predicting positive school attitudes and few problem behaviors, even after controlling for parental religious involvement. Youniss, McLellan, and Yates[68] review data that demonstrate the significance of religion to identity formation. They linked religious involvement to increased community service activity, religious ideology, and greater school engagement, all of which subsequently facilitate healthy identity development.

Theoretically, religious institutions help facilitate the management and interpretation of difficult experiences and skills necessary for navigating in the larger society. Historically, black churches have been instrumental in instilling a sense of God (spiritual understanding), self, history, and community in addition to building character, self-esteem, and unity. As Lincoln[69] states, "In the African American experience . . . [religious] belief(s) and practice was sufficiently common to the African American mini-cultures to provide a framework of reference from which a common identity could reasonably be inferred" (p. 219). The black church became the chief index of identification, not because it transcended "race-rooted . . . values and behaviors" but because it was an opportunity to express, transmit, and validate cultural identity. This type of socialization process as linked with cultural identity has also been found among other ethnic minority populations. For example, Bankston and Zhou[70] noted that religious participation in Vietnamese immigrants significantly contributed to ethnic identity among adolescent high school students. They further attributed positive adjustment of these youth into the larger society to the opportunity they have for cultivating a distinct ethnicity.

This integration is salient in the second decade of life. Adolescents' cognitive sophistication in exploring answers to complex issues cannot be addressed through the church as a context for social interaction or through commitment to a denomination.[71] It is the essence or foundation of what these terms represent that is the heart of spirituality. Church attendance alone is merely an exercise or ritual, if the accompanying ideals are not integrated into the individual's sense of self. This integration presents a framework for understanding and navigating one's world, particularly as a minority member. In essence, one's framework is not obtained solely through church participation but rather through a belief structure that is potentially nurtured by participation in traditional church activities. Organized church activities offer a context for connectedness and exploration of oneself as a vital member of society.[72] Although researchers have suggested that African American families rely on the church as an institution of support far less now than ever before,[73] there remains a strong connection to the values and beliefs associated with ongoing church attendance. Just as spirituality has promoted validation of strength and integrity regarding one's minority status, it has also been a framework for interpreting and coping with life events.

Conclusions

We have looked at race and gender identity for African American youth and examined schools and religious institutions as a context of risk and protection. Using the PVEST framework, we see how identity and context interplay in normative development. It is evident that this interaction has implications for efforts to promote positive youth development and to understand less productive outcomes. We have emphasized particular domains to illustrate PVEST and its utility, but our work spans multiple contexts (school, neighborhood, and family) and various domains of identity, including career and academic identities along with race and gender. Human development is the complex interaction of all of these domains of human functioning and contexts as lives unfold over time.

A thorough understanding of resilience and positive outcomes can only come from careful, conceptually driven analysis of this interaction. This strategy allows customization of supports for maximizing positive youth development. As an explanatory conceptual framework focusing on life-course human development, PVEST gives us an ideal means to accomplish this end.

Notes

1. Spencer, M. B. (1995). Old issues and new theorizing about African American youth: A phenomenological variant of ecological systems theory. In R. L. Taylor (Ed.), *Black youth: Perspectives on their status in the United States* (pp. 37–70). Westport, CT: Praeger.

2. Ibid.

3. Ibid.

4. Bronfenbrenner, U. (1989). Ecological systems theory. In R. Vasta (Ed.), *Annals of child development* (pp. 187–248). Greenwich, CT: JAI.

5. Spencer (1995); Spencer, M. B., Dupree, D., & Hartmann, T. (1997). A phenomenological variant of ecological systems theory (PVEST): A self-organization perspective in context. *Development and Psychopathology, 9*(4), 817–833; Spencer, M. B. (1999). Social and cultural influences on school adjustment: The application of an identity-focused cultural ecological perspective. *Educational Psychologist, 34*(1), 43–57.

6. Spencer (1995).

7. Bronfenbrenner (1989).

8. Stevenson, H. C. (1997). "Missed, dissed, and pissed": Making meaning of neighborhood risk, fear and anger management in urban black youth. *Cultural Diversity and Mental Health, 3*(1), 37–52.

9. Erikson, E. (1968). *Identity: Youth and crisis.* New York: Norton.

10. Ogbu, J. (1985). A cultural ecology of competence among inner-city blacks. In M. B. Spencer, G. K. Brookins, & W. R. Allen (Eds.), *Beginnings: The social and affective development of black children* (pp. 45–66). Mahwah, NJ: Erlbaum.

11. Spencer, M. B., & Dupree, D. (1996). African American youths' eco-cultural challenges and psychosocial opportunities: An alternative analysis of problem behavior outcomes. In D. Cicchetti & S. Toth (Eds.), *Rochester Symposium on Developmental Psychopathology: Vol. 7. Adolescence: Opportunities and challenges* (pp. 259–282). Rochester, NY: University of Rochester Press.

12. Bandura, A. (1978). The self system in reciprocal determinism. *American Psychologist, 33,* 344–358.

13. Spencer, M. B., Swanson, D. P., & Cunningham, M. (1991). Ethnicity, ethnic identity and competence formation: Adolescent transition and identity transformation. *Journal of Negro Education, 60*(3), 366–387.

14. Havighurst, R. J. (1953). *Human development and education.* New York: McKay.

15. Ruble, D. N. (1988). Sex-role development. In M. H. Bornstein & M. E. Lamb (Eds.), *Developmental psychology: An advanced textbook* (2nd ed., pp. 411–459). Mahwah, NJ: Erlbaum.

16. Cunningham, M. (1993). African American adolescent males sex role development. *Journal of African American Males Studies, 1*(1), 30–37; Ketterlinus, R., & Lamb, M. E. (1994). *Adolescent problem behaviors.* Mahwah, NJ: Erlbaum.

17. Spencer, M. B. (2001). Identity, achievement, orientation and race: "Lessons learned" about the normative developmental experiences of African American males. In W. Watkins, J. H. Lewis, & V. Chou (Eds.), *Race and education* (pp. 100–127). Needham Heights, MA: Allyn & Bacon.

18. Harris, S. M., Gold, S. R., & Henderson, B. B. (1991). Relationships between

achievement and affiliation needs and sex-role orientation of college women whose fathers were absent from home. *Perceptual and Motor Skills, 72,* 1307–1315.

19. Ladner, J. A. (1972). *Tomorrow's tomorrow: The black woman.* New York: Doubleday.

20. Swanson, D. P., & Spencer, M. B. (1997). Developmental considerations of gender-linked attributes during adolescence. In R. D. Taylor & M. C. Wang (Eds.), *Social and emotional adjustment and family relations in ethnic minority families* (pp. 181–199). Mahwah, NJ: Erlbaum.

21. Spencer (1999); Spencer (2001).

22. Spencer, M. B., Cunningham, M., & Swanson, D. P. (1995). Identity as coping: Adolescent African American males' adaptive responses to high risk environments. In H. W. Harris, H. C. Blue, and E. H. Griffith (Eds.), *Racial and ethnic identity* (pp. 31–52). New York: Routledge.

23. Spencer, M. B. (1990). Parental values transmission: Implications for black child development. In J. B. Stewart & H. Cheathan (Eds.), *Interdisciplinary perspectives on black families* (pp. 111–130). New Brunswick, NJ: Transaction; Spencer, M. B. (1983). Children's cultural values and parental child rearing strategies. *Developmental Review, 3,* 351–370.

24. Spencer (1999).

25. Hill, J. P., & Lynch, M. E. (1983). The intensification of gender-related role expectations during early adolescence. In J. Brooks-Gunn & A. C. Petersen (Eds.), *Girls at puberty: Biological and psychosocial perspectives* (pp.201–228). New York: Plenum.

26. Spencer, M. B., Dupree, D., Swanson, D., & Cunningham, M. (1996). Parental monitoring and adolescents' sense of responsibility for their own learning: An examination of sex differences. *Journal of Negro Education, 65*(1), 30–43.

27. Jung, C. (1993). Cognitive mediators of aggression in hyperactive, aggressive, and hyperactive-aggressive children. Unpublished doctoral dissertation, University of Calgary, Alberta, Canada.

28. Weist, M., Freedman, A., Paskwitz, D., Jackson, C., Flaherty, L., & Proescher, E. (1995). Urban youth under stress: Empirical identification of risk and resilience factors. *Journal of Youth and Adolescence, 24,* 705–721.

29. Swanson, D. P., & Spencer, M. B. (1997). Developmental considerations of gender-linked attributes during adolescence. In R. D. Taylor & M. C. Wang (Eds.), *Social and emotional adjustment and family relations in ethnic minority families* (pp. 181–199). Mahwah, NJ: Erlbaum.

30. Hill, H. M., Levermore, M., Twaite, J., & Jones, L. P. (1996). Exposure to community violence and social support as predictors of anxiety and social and emotional behavior among African American children. *Journal of Child and Family Studies, 5,* 399–414.

31. Grunberg, N. E., & Straub, R. O. (1992). The role of gender and taste class in the effects of stress on eating. *Health Psychology, 11*(2), 97–100.

32. Michaud, C. I., Kahn, J., Musse, N., Burlet, C., Nicolas, J., Mejean, L. (1990). Relationships between a critical life event and eating behaviour in high school students. *Stress Medicine, 6,* 57–64; Greeno, C. G., & Wing, R. R. (1994). Stress-induced eating. *Psychological Bulletin, 115*(3), 444–464.

33. Striegel-Moore, R. H., Garvin, V., Dohm, F.-A., & Rosenheck, R. (1999). Eating disorders in a national sample of hospitalized female and male

veterans: Prevalence and psychiatric comorbidity. *International Journal of Eating Disorders, 25*, 405–414.

34. Parker, S., Nichter, M., Nichter, M., Vuckovic, N., Sims, C., & Ritenbaugh, C. (1995). Body image and weight concerns among African American and white adolescent females: Differences that make a difference. *Human Organization, 54*(2), 103–113.

35. Bronfenbrenner (1989).

36. Erikson (1968).

37. White, R. (1960). Competence and psychosexual development. In M. R. Jones (Ed.), *Nebraska Symposium on Motivation* (pp. 3–32). Lincoln: University of Nebraska Press.

38. Swanson, D. P., & Spencer, M. B. (1998). Developmental and cultural context considerations for research on African American adolescents (pp. 53–72). In H. E. Fitzgerald, B. M. Lester, & B. Zuckerman (Eds.), *Children of color: Research, health, and public policy issues*. Chicago: University of Chicago Press.

39. Obiakor, F. E., Grant, P. A., and Dooley, E. A.(2002). *Educating all learners: Refocusing the comprehensive support model*. Springfield, IL: Charles C. Thomas Publishers.

40. Swanson and Spencer (1998).

41. Jencks, C., & Mayer, S. (1990). The social consequences of growing up in a poor neighborhood. In L. E. Lynn, Jr., & M.G.H. McGeary (Eds.), *Inner city poverty in the United States* (pp. 111–186). Washington, DC: National Academy Press.

42. Spencer (1999).

43. Bennett, C. K., & Bennett, J. A. (1994, Apr.). Teachers' attributions and beliefs in relation to gender and success of students. Paper presented at the Annual Meeting of the American Educational Research Association, New Orleans.

44. Marwit, S. J. (1982). Students' race, physical attractiveness, and teacher's judgements of transgressions: Follow-up and clarification. *Psychological Reports, 50*, 242.

45. DeMeis, D. K, & Turner, R. R. (1978). Effects of students' race, physical attractiveness, and dialect on teachers' evaluations. *Contemporary Educational Psychology, 3*(1), 77–86.

46. Harber, K. D. (1998). Feedback to minorities: Evidence of a positive bias. *Journal of Personality and Social Psychology, 74*(3), 622–628.

47. Ibid.

48. Adams, G. R., & Cohen, A. S. (1976). Characteristics of children and teacher expectancy: An extension to the child's social and family life. *Journal of Educational Research, 70*, 87–90.

49. Brophy, J. (1985). Teacher's expectations, motives and goals for working with problem students. In C. Ames & R. E. Ames (Eds.), *Research on motivation in education: The classroom milieu* (vol. 2, pp. 175–214). Orlando: Academic Press; Dusek, J. B., and Dusek, J. G. (1985). *Teacher expectancies*. Mahwah, NJ: Erlbaum.

50. Dusek and Dusek (1985).

51. Brophy (1985).

52. Dusek and Dusek (1985).

53. Cooper, H., & Good, T. (1983). *Pygmalion grows up: Studies in the expectation communication process*. White Plains, NY: Longman.

54. Spencer, Dupree, & Hartmann (1997).

55. Fordham, S., & Ogbu, J. U. (1986). Black students' school success: Coping with the "burden of 'acting white.'" *Urban Review, 18*(3), 176–206.

56. Spencer, M. B., Noll, E., Stoltzfus, J., & Harpalani, V. (2001). Identity and school adjustment: Revisiting the "acting white" assumption. *Educational Psychologist, 36*(1), 21–30.

57. Spencer, M. B., & Dornbush, S. (1990). Challenges in studying minority youth. In S. Feldman & G. Elliott (Eds.), *At the threshold: The developing adolescent* (pp. 123–146). Cambridge, MA: Harvard University Press; Spencer, Swanson, & Cunningham (1991).

58. Ogbu (1985).

59. Spencer, M. B. (1988). Self-concept development. In D. T. Slaughter (Ed.), *Perspectives on black child development: New directions for child development* (pp. 59–72). San Francisco: Jossey-Bass.

60. Chestang, L. W. (1972). Character development in a hostile environment. Occasional Paper Series, no. 3 (pp. 1–12). Chicago: University of Chicago.

61. Fowler, J. W. (1981). *Stages of faith: The psychology of human development and the quest for faith.* New York: HarperCollins.

62. Swanson, D. P., Spencer, M. B., & Petersen, A. (1998). Adolescent identity formation: 21st century issues and opportunities. In K. M. Borman & B. Schneider (Eds.), *Youth experiences and development: Social influences and educational challenges.* Chicago: University of Chicago Press.

63. Donelson, E. (1999). Psychology of religion and adolescents in the United States: Past to present. *Journal of Adolescence, 22,* 187–204; Weaver, A. J., Samford, J. A., Morgan, V. J., Lichton, A. I., Larson, D. B., & Garbarino, J. (2000). Research on religious variables in five major adolescent research journals: 1992 to 1996. *Journal of Nervous and Mental Disease, 188,* 36–44.

64. Amey, C. H, Albrecht, S. L, & Miller, M. K. (1996). Racial differences in adolescent drug use: The impact of religion. *Substance Use and Misuse, 31,* 1311–1332.

65. Benda, B. B. (1995). The effect of religion on adolescent delinquency revisited. *Journal of Research in Crime and Delinquency, 32,* 446–466.

66. Meyer, A. L., & Lausell, L. (1996). The value of including a "higher power" in efforts to prevent violence and promote optimal outcomes during adolescence. In R. L. Hampton, P. Jenkins, & T. P. Gullotta (Eds.), *Preventing violence in America: Issues in children's and families' lives* (vol. 4, pp. 115–132). Thousand Oaks, CA: Sage.

67. Trusty, J., & Watts, R. E. (1999). Relationship of high school seniors' religious perceptions and behavior to educational, career, and leisure variables. *Counseling and Values, 44,* 30–39.

68. Youniss, J., McLellan, J. A., & Yates, M. (1999). Religion, community service, and identity in American youth. *Journal of Adolescence, 22,* 243–253.

69. Lincoln, E. C. (1995). Black religion and racial identity. In H. W. Harris, H. C. Blue, & E.E.H. Griffith (Eds.), *Racial and ethnic identity: Psychological development and creative expression* (pp. 208–221). New York: Routledge.

70. Bankston, C. L, & Zhou, M. (1995). Religious participation, ethnic identification, and adaptation of Vietnamese adolescents in an immigrant community. *Sociological Quarterly, 36,* 523–534.

71. Keating, D. P. (1990). Adolescent thinking. In S. S. Feldman & G. R. Elliott (Eds.), *At the threshold: The developing adolescent* (pp. 54–89). Cambridge, MA: Harvard University Press.

72. Holder, D. W., Durant, R. H., Harris, T. L., Daniel, J. H., Obeidallah, D., & Goodman, E. (2000). The association between adolescent spirituality and voluntary sexual activity. *Journal of Adolescent Health, 26,* 295–302.

73. McAdoo, H. P. (1992). Upward mobility and parenting in middle-income black families. In A. K. Burlew, W. C. Banks, H. P. McAdoo, & D. A. Azibo (Eds.), *African American psychology: Theory, research and practice* (pp. 63–86). Thousand Oaks, CA: Sage; Walker, K., Taylor, E., McElroy, A., Phillip, D., & Wilson, M. N. (1995). Familial and ecological correlates of self-esteem in African American children. In M. N. Wilson (Ed.), *African American family life: Its structural and ecological aspects.* New Directions for Child Development (pp. 23–34). San Francisco: Jossey-Bass; Wilson, M. N. (1989). Child development in the context of the black extended family. *American Psychologist, 44,* 380–385.

DENA PHILLIPS SWANSON *is assistant professor in the College of Health and Human Development, Pennsylvania State University.*

MARGARET BEALE SPENCER *is the GSE Board of Overseers Professor of Education, professor of psychology at the University of Pennsylvania, and director of the Center for Health Achievement Neighborhood Growth and Ethnic Studies and the W.E.B. Du Bois Collective Research Institute.*

TABITHA DELL'ANGELO *is a doctoral candidate in the Graduate School of Education, University of Pennsylvania.*

VINAY HARPALANI *is a doctoral candidate in the Graduate School of Education and a master of bioethics candidate in the School of Medicine, University of Pennsylvania.*

TIRZAH R. SPENCER *holds a master's in public health and is a doctoral candidate in the College of Health and Human Development, Pennsylvania State University.*

Within the context of a developmental psychopathology model emphasizing person-context transactions across the life span, adjustment disturbances among youth in upper-class suburbia are discussed. Potential reasons for these problems, involving achievement pressure and disconnection from parents, are explored.

5

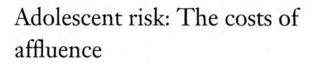

Adolescent risk: The costs of affluence

Suniya S. Luthar, Shawn J. Latendresse

DEVELOPMENTAL SCIENTISTS have increasingly emphasized the limits to any one-model-fits-all perspective that is based on patterns observed in the mainstream of middle-class youth. Accordingly, the last few years have witnessed an increase in context-sensitive theoretical and empirical efforts focused on economically disadvantaged and minority children.[1] At the same time, there has been little empirical attention to the unique life experiences of youngsters at the opposite end of the socioeconomic spectrum, that is, children in highly affluent, upwardly mobile families.

The importance of context-sensitive research on affluent youth is evident in recent suggestions of manifest adjustment problems

Note: Preparation of the manuscript was supported in part by grants from the National Institutes of Health (RO1-DA10726 and RO1-DA11498), the William T. Grant Foundation, and the Spencer Foundation. Further information about this research can be obtained from Suniya S. Luthar, Department of Human Development, Columbia University Teachers College, Box 133, 525 120th St., New York, NY 10027.

NEW DIRECTIONS FOR YOUTH DEVELOPMENT, NO. 95, FALL 2002 © WILEY PERIODICALS, INC.

among the rich. In a recent special issue of the *American Psychologist*, several scholars argued that material wealth can be inversely related to psychological well-being. Reviewing cross-national epidemiological data, Buss[2] noted that rates of depressive disorders, which have increased in recent years, are higher in more economically developed countries. Considering the United States specifically, historical trends show that Americans today have more luxuries than they had decades ago yet are no happier than they used to be.[3] On the basis of data spanning 1958 to 1998, Meyers wrote, "We are twice as rich and no happier. Meanwhile, the divorce rate doubled. Teen suicide tripled. . . . Depression rates have soared, especially among teens and young adults. . . . I call this conjunction of material prosperity and social recession *the American paradox*. The more people strive for extrinsic goals such as money, the more numerous their problems and the less robust their well being."[4]

Inverse links between affluence and well-being have been explained in terms of various underlying mechanisms, including individuals' rapid habituation to new wealth, envy of people with the most luxuries, and isolation spawned by resolute pursuit of personal ambitions. Following Brickman and Campbell's suggestion[5] that people tend to labor on a "hedonic treadmill," several scholars have argued that when individuals strive for a certain level of affluence and reach it, they become quickly habituated and then start wanting the next level of material success.[6] Others have noted that in relatively affluent communities, depression can derive from self-perceived failure arising when people compare their own circumstances with the exorbitantly successful, glamorous lifestyles depicted in mass communications.[7] Yet another argument rests on the relative anonymity and dearth of informal supports that characterize modern living conditions in many affluent communities, factors that in turn engender feelings of alienation and loneliness among inhabitants.[8] Finally, the pursuit of affluence and fame often runs counter to attaining socioemotional rewards. At the most concrete level, long work hours reduce leisure time. At a psychological level, as Csikszentmihalyi has noted, ". . .to the extent that most of one's psychic energy becomes invested in material goals, it is typical for sensitivity to other rewards to atrophy."[9] Empirical evidence on material versus socioemotional goals is consistent with this argument: individuals who place high value on occupational success and prestige relative to gratifying personal lives have been found to be at escalated risk for emotional distress.[10]

So far, there have been few investigations of the degree to which such trends noted among affluent adults generalize to children, but the little evidence that exists does suggest similarities. In a sample of almost one thousand American teens, Csikszentmihalyi and Schneider[11] found a low negative relationship between parents' social class and teenagers' well-being. Children in the lowest socioeconomic strata reported the highest happiness, and the most affluent children reported the least happiness. Additionally, there have been suggestions that parent-adolescent connections can become increasingly compromised as the demanding lives of professional parents impinge upon critical "family time."[12] A recent national survey by the U.S. Department of Health and Human Services[13] has in fact revealed that closeness to parents tends to be inversely related to household income, among adolescents aged twelve to seventeen.

Although inquiry into facets of psychological adjustment among affluent youth is only just beginning, several studies have already indicated their heightened vulnerability to substance use. Data from the national Monitoring the Future study, for example, have shown that during preadolescence and early adolescence, family socioeconomic status (SES) has a low association with the use of most drugs. By the twelfth grade, on the other hand, upper-SES youth reflect the highest rate of several substances, including marijuana, inhalants, and tranquilizers.[14] Similarly, a statewide survey of youth in Connecticut, based on a sample of more than twelve thousand students,[15] indicated that among high school students the highest level of smoking and drinking occurred in the top two of the nine SES groups.

Adding to concern about suburban teens' substance use is recent evidence on the increasing popularity of "club drugs" (such as

MDMA, Ketamine, and Rohypnol), which are frequently used by the relatively affluent. The National Institute on Drug Abuse[16] reported that between the years 1998 and 1999 there was a significant increase in the use of MDMA, or "ecstasy," with the percentage of lifetime use among twelfth graders increasing from 5.8 percent to 8.0 percent, and an increase in monthly use from 1.5 percent to 2.5 percent. These increases are alarming given the potential of these drugs to cause serious health problems, including death, especially in combination with alcohol.[17]

Studies by our research group

Over the last ten years, research by our group has yielded incremental evidence that is resonant with previously noted suggestions of problems among affluent youth. Major findings of these studies are presented in the discussions that follow. Methodologically, a common feature across all these investigations is a rigorous assessment approach involving multiple methods, multiple informants, and psychometrically sound measures.

Conceptually, our consideration of vulnerability and protective factors has been guided by a developmental psychopathology conceptual model, entailing emphasis on the importance of transactions among contexts, as well as the ontogenetic coherence of development. Specifically, our work is guided by theories emphasizing transactions between ecological contexts and the developing child, such as Bronfenbrenner's ecological theory,[18] Sameroff and Chandler's transactional perspective,[19] and Cicchetti and Lynch's ecological-transactional model of development.[20] Across all of these theories, the phrase *ecological context* refers not only to relatively proximal context such as the family and school but also to the broader cultural milieu within which the child develops. A cardinal premise is that development occurs within the framework of an integrated system, entailing transactions among aspects of the child's development and different levels of the ecological surround. Secondly, our work reflects the structural-organizational perspective,[21] central to which is the belief that there is continuity in the unfolding of competence over time. Although manifestations of competence vary across the developmental span (depending on the relevant stage-salient tasks, for example), coherence is typically maintained in an individual's competence patterns ontogenetically. These broad developmental psychopathology principles form the organizing framework for all aspects of the research studies that we present here.

Early research with inner-city adolescents

Our programmatic research on social competence and psychopathology among adolescents began with studies of youth in poverty, with a central focus on the construct of resilience.[22] Major questions addressed concentrated on the factors that might explain why some youth facing high life stress do relatively well on major age-salient tasks (that is, those reflecting what society expects for children of that age). Outcome domains of major interest included adolescents' capacities to get along well with both peers and adults (respectively indexed by ratings by peers and teachers at school), as well as levels of academic performance.

Over the course of several investigations, among the most intriguing of insights we obtained were those involving high status in the peer group. In general, peer ratings of sociability tend to be linked with positive school behavior among children.[23] On the other hand, we found links in the opposite direction within our adolescent, inner-city sample. High sociability showed significant cross-sectional links with peer ratings of disruptive, aggressive behaviors, suggesting that this teenage peer group was somewhat admiring of individuals who had the gumption to buck the system. Similarly, we found negative prospective links with academic performance. Students who were popular early in the year were likely to show significant declines in grades over time, again suggesting that the peer group disdained what was valued by "the establishment."

In appraising these findings, we recognized that they could have represented essentially an inner-city phenomenon, or more broadly an adolescent one. Thus, the research question to be addressed next was, If the peer group did endorse behavioral nonconformity, was this something restricted to the ecology of urban poverty, or something characterizing adolescents more generally?

Comparisons: Inner-city and suburban youth

To address this question, we located a group that was quite different in socioeconomic terms from the inner-city group. We sampled youngsters living in relatively affluent, mostly white-collar professional families in a suburb in the northeastern United States. This comparative study[24] involved almost 500 students in the tenth grade, 264 in the suburban high school and 224 in the inner-city school. There were approximately equal numbers of boys and girls in both schools. The suburban sample was largely Caucasian, and the inner-city sample predominantly minority; use of free or reduced lunch applied to 1 percent and 86 percent of students respectively in the two schools. With regard to methods, as in our prior research on resilience and vulnerability, we used multi-informant, multitrait assessments to measure various aspects of self-reported problems, as well as academic records and ratings of behavioral competence by both peers and teachers.

In comparing *levels of self-reported problems* for the two groups, we found that collectively these were significantly higher among the suburban students.[25] Affluent youth reported significantly higher levels of anxiety across several domains, and levels of depressive symptoms were marginally higher. They also reported significantly higher levels of substance use, with consistently higher use of cigarettes, alcohol, marijuana, and any illicit drug.

We also appraised these adjustment difficulties in comparison with national normative data; here again, we had some startling findings. To illustrate, among suburban girls in the tenth grade, one in five reported clinically significant depression, a rate three times as high as those among normative samples. Rates of clinically significant anxiety among both girls and boys in the suburban high school were also somewhat higher than normative values (22 percent and 26 percent, versus 17 percent).[26]

Similar patterns were seen on indices of substance use. With the exception of cigarettes, use of all other substances was higher among suburban youth as compared to national norms, with particularly striking elevation in use of alcohol among girls (72 percent versus 61 percent [norms]) and any illicit drug use among boys (59 percent versus 38 percent).

Examination of significant *correlates of adolescents' substance use* showed that among suburban youth, but not their inner-city counterparts, substance use was significantly linked with indicators of self-reported maladjustment.[27] Consistent with theories of "self-medication," therefore, it appeared that suburban youth, more so than inner-city teens, may have used substances to alleviate personal distress. Notably, similar findings have been reported in qualitative research comparing youth from high and low socioeconomic backgrounds.[28]

Data from our comparative study also showed that among boys in the affluent community—but not inner-city boys, or either subgroup of girls—peers seemed to endorse high substance use. Suburban boys' popularity with peers (indexed by peer nominations on "Who do you like most"?) had significant positive links with high substance use. No links were found between peer rejection (nominations on "like least") and substance use. Furthermore, the link between suburban boys' peer popularity and their substance use remained significant despite statistical controls for various related indices that could have operated as confounds (level of depression, anxiety, delinquency, teacher-rated classroom behaviors). [29]

Among girls in the suburban school, both peer acceptance and peer rejection were linked with substance use, but the magnitude of the associations was lower than those previously described for boys' peer acceptance. Furthermore, neither remained significant after statistically controlling for other adjustment indices that could have been confounds.

Prospective analyses on suburban high school youth

Faced with the many signs of trouble in our cross-sectional data— collected when our suburban students were in the tenth grade— we followed these students through the rest of their stay in high school, to assess the continuity of problems and to examine potential pathways to maladjustment and competence. Although this research was not originally planned to be longitudinal in design, we were successful in collecting data on almost 90 percent of the original sample of students in reassessing them as seniors, approximately two and a half years later.

The levels of internalizing problems were generally stable across this two-year period, although there was some increases among girls in the sample. To illustrate, almost 22 percent of suburban girls had been above the clinical cutoff for depressive symptoms as tenth graders, and 19 percent were above cutoffs as twelfth graders. On anxiety, incidence of clinically significant symptoms among girls increased over time, from one in five to almost one in three by the end of high school.

With regard to *substance use* between the tenth and twelfth grades, the incidence of heavy drinking (to intoxication) and of marijuana use increased over time among both girls and boys. Whereas 62 percent of girls and 58 percent of boys reported never having drunk to intoxication during the tenth grade, 40 percent of girls and 37 percent of boys reported this as high school seniors. Similarly, complete abstention from marijuana use over the past year was reported by 60 percent of girls and 62 percent of boys in the tenth grade, but only 40 percent of girls and 50 percent of boys during grade twelve.

Using longitudinal data, we then examined cross-sectional findings[30] on potential *antecedents of substance use*. Multiple regression analyses were conducted with statistical controls for baseline substance use scores.[31] These stringent analyses allowed us to examine whether adjustment indicators at baseline were linked with an increase in substance use, considering a period of more than two years. Results indicated that high physiological anxiety at baseline was significantly linked with increases in both cigarette and alcohol use, supporting earlier cross-sectional findings suggesting self-medication. In addition, boys with high peer status showed significant increases in their use of alcohol over time, suggesting social conformity effects on drinking among adolescent males.

We also examined links in the opposite direction, namely, *potential psychosocial consequences of substance use* among these youth. In this case, results showed that among girls, early substance use presaged heightened maladjustment in externalizing and internalizing problems (delinquency, social and physiological anxiety), possibly reflecting the high deviance of excessive substance use among girls. Among boys, use of alcohol and marijuana were each prospectively linked with a single outcome domain—teacher-rated classroom disruptiveness—reflecting heterotypic continuity of their counter-conventional behaviors.

In summary, our research with high school students revealed that teens in wealthy suburban families reported higher distress and substance use than did other youth of the same age but from modest economic backgrounds. Furthermore, we found that high distress may often be implicated in substance use among affluent teens but not their inner-city counterparts, and also that peer approval may be a salient factor, particularly in suburban boys' levels of alcohol use. Finally, our data suggests some bidirectionality in association between substance use and other adjustment indicators; high substance use seemed to presage increased problems in multiple adjustment domains among girls, and in disruptive classroom behaviors among suburban boys.

Middle school youth: A cross-sectional survey

Around the time we first obtained evidence of distress among upper-SES high school youth,[32] the first author of this article was coincidentally asked to consult to middle schools in a nearby community, also affluent. Following a rash of incidents involving substance use among their middle school students, administrators and PTA representatives sought to determine the magnitude of this and related problems, as well as potential causes. Accordingly, we surveyed all sixth and seventh graders in one of the two middle schools in this town ($n = 320$), tapping into not only major adjustment indices but also their potential antecedents.

With regard to incidence of adjustment difficulties, these cross-sectional data indicated that at the sixth grade level both depressive and anxiety symptoms were at or below normative levels. Among students in the seventh grade, however, elevations were observed in both, particularly among girls. Similarly, these data showed that substance use was negligible among sixth graders but was beginning among seventh graders. To illustrate, 7 percent of boys reported having drunk until intoxicated or tried marijuana at least once a month on average, whereas no boys or girls in the sixth grade had done so.

Potential antecedents of maladjustment

In beginning to explore possible antecedents of distress of suburban youth, we focused on two major indices: achievement pressures and disconnection from parents.[33] The first of these was examined because of prior suggestions that in upwardly mobile, affluent communities there is often pervasive emphasis on ensuring the success of children across virtually all domains of competence, pressures that drive youth to try to excel at academics as well as multiple extracurricular activities.[34] The resultant potential for maladjustment is evident in previous findings that, among preadolescents and teens from diverse backgrounds, pressures to achieve at school are linked with various forms of maladjustment.[35]

In considering achievement pressures, we sought to operationalize these in terms of children's perception of their parents' emphasis on achievement, as well as their own internalized drive to excel. At the time we initiated this research, we were unable to locate a measure of the former, that is, children's perception of the degree to which their parents emphasized their accomplishment as opposed to aspects of their personal development. We therefore created a measure of perceived parental values.[36] Students were presented with a set of ten issues potentially important to all parents, and asked to rank-order those perceived as the top five in terms of what their parents would value the most. Half of these values pertained to achievement (such as academic excellence and attending a good college in the future). The other half represented personal character and well-being, such as emphasis on respectfulness or helpfulness to others.

Latent class analyses based on ranking revealed three meaningful clusters, one of which consisted of students who saw their parents as valuing their achievement highly, and the other two consisting of children whose parents valued their personal character and well-being. Validity of these classes was evident in the significant differences obtained on an independent questionnaire on high parental expectations, wherein differences between the clusters indicated medium to large effect size, in expected directions.

To measure the second dimension of achievement pressure, we used the Multidimensional Perfectionism Scale,[37] which assesses both adaptive and maladaptive dimensions of internalized drives to perform and succeed. The second of these dimensions was included in our analyses; this represented unreasonably high perfectionistic tendencies, as reflected, for example, in children's high doubts and concern over mistakes made in achievement-related tasks.

The second major construct considered as an antecedent of suburban youth's distress was disconnection from adults. Like achievement pressure, this was examined in terms of two indicators: emotional connection and physical presence. The former was operationalized by composite variables of emotional closeness (feelings of trust, communication, and involvement), with mothers and fathers considered separately. For the latter, we asked about after-school supervision, meaning, whether or not children were regularly supervised by an adult after school hours.

In examining the role of these various socializing indices in relation to children's distress, we first considered, within all statistical analyses, the possible effects of a diffuse or generalized tendency toward negative affect, as this might artificially inflate links between children's perceived problems with parents and their own self-reported maladjustment. The construct used to rule out such confounds was children's reports of negative experiences in relationships with their peers. This was entered into all regression equations before considering effects of the major predictors, namely, student reports of excessive achievement pressure and of isolation from parents.

With regard to adjustment outcomes in these analyses, we considered a composite variable of internal distress, which represented symptoms of both depression and anxiety (these were highly correlated). In addition, a composite substance use variable based on combined frequency of cigarettes and alcohol[38] was created. In supplementary analyses, we considered school grades as an outcome variable, given the possibility that high achievement pressures may in fact promote high academic scores among suburban youth even as they might engender high levels of personal distress among them. Results of analyses were as follows:

- In predicting inner distress, even after considering perceived victimization by peers, maladaptive perfectionism had strong links among all groups, with pronounced associations among sixth and seventh grade girls.
- Distress was also linked with parent values among seventh grade girls, with lack of after-school supervision among both boys and girls in the seventh grade, and with closeness to both parents among sixth grade boys and seventh grade girls.
- There were relatively few associations with substance use at the sixth grade (unsurprising, given the low substance use in this group).
- However, substance use was related to maladaptive perfectionism and low closeness to mother among seventh grade boys, and to lack of after-school supervision and low closeness to mother among seventh grade girls.
- Whereas perceived achievement pressures were clearly linked with students' self-reported distress, they did not show any associations with academic grades. Thus there was no evidence that adults' high emphasis on achievement actually engendered academic success.

Obviously, none of these findings permit any conclusions about causality, or about age-related changes in associations, given their basis in cross-sectional data. Collectively, however, they do substantiate the relevance of the constructs used as possible antecedents of adjustment difficulties within the suburban context. We expect that the magnitude of predicted associations will be incrementally stronger as children negotiate the adolescent years, given not only the increases in symptoms of depression, anxiety, and substance use over the course of adolescence (reducing restricted range of outcomes) but also the likely heightened significance of achievement issues (for example, with the crystallization of ambitions within the adolescent's developing sense of identity,[39] as well as the approach of the highly competitive process of seeking and procuring admission to a reputed university).

Distress among affluent children: Merely vicissitudes of adolescence?

Previously described findings of high self-reported problems among suburban teenagers might be viewed as benign by some, for at least two reasons. One is that they could reflect patterns that are developmentally normative. Adolescence has historically been characterized as a period of storm and stress,[40] and studies have established that the teen years generate more mood and conduct disturbance than does either childhood or adulthood.[41] Similarly, Zucker and his colleagues[42] have described a developmentally limited pattern of substance use wherein the incidence of heavy drinking increases during adolescence but then diminishes over time, with many young adults "maturing out" of excessive use of alcohol.[43]

A second relevant issue is the presence of "safety nets" or systems of support that tend to accompany higher socioeconomic status; these could help to alleviate the adjustment problems of affluent youth over time. Environments such as these are often rich in resources such as good schools, good mental health services, and parents and teachers with a strong investment in pulling adolescents toward conforming to mainstream mores.[44]

Offsetting these considerations are at least two factors arguing against too sanguine an outlook, the first of which stems from comparison of suburban youth with other sociodemographic groups of the same age. To reiterate, the first of our studies[45] showed that affluent teens reported substantially higher levels of substance use, anxiety symptoms, and depressive problems as compared with both inner-city youth and national normative samples. Second, prior research evidence has established that problems such as these can have serious long-term sequelae, in terms of within-domain continuity as well as spillover effects to other domains. For example, the incidence of anxiety or depressive disorders during adolescence is associated with a twofold or threefold increase in risk for the same problems during adulthood.[46] Additionally, high subjective emotional distress can inhibit an individual's ability to maintain adequate functioning across various spheres including academic and job performance, behavioral conformity, and interpersonal relationships; there is also evidence of substantial effects on physical health status.[47] With regard to substance use, research has shown that almost 40 percent of those who eventually develop alcohol use disorders manifest their first symptoms between the ages of fifteen and nineteen years.[48] Furthermore, substance use among suburban teens is often of the "negative affect" type[49]—associated with depressive and anxious symptomatology[50]—a subtype with relatively high continuity of problems over time.[51] Finally, long-term disturbances across various domains can derive from problems of substance use, ranging from educational, occupational, and social difficulties to traumatic injury and rape.[52]

Collectively, factors such as these indicate the value of longitudinal research to examine the degree to which suburban adolescents' distress and substance use represent temporary blips in otherwise healthy trajectories, as opposed to representing a serious problem at least in some instances. We are currently engaged in such a study, following a group of affluent youth over seven annual waves from sixth grade through the end of high school. This research could be critical in illuminating the stability or variability of outcomes across time as well as the real-world ramifications of problems previously documented.

To summarize, our research findings with suburban middle school students were generally resonant with those we previously obtained with high school students. Cross-sectional data suggested that by the seventh grade level, affluent, suburban youngsters may begin to show some elevation in depressive and anxiety symptoms as well as substance use, compared to national normative samples. Our initial efforts to understand contextually salient risk factors showed that in these settings, high achievement pressures and feelings of isolation from parents may be salient in contributing to children's maladjustment. Although the adjustment problems we have documented could partially reflect adolescent-specific angst, it is premature to simply presume that they will remit by the end of the teen years. Longitudinal research spanning preadolescence through early adulthood is necessary to help gauge the overall seriousness of the types of difficulties suggested by existing empirical studies.

Research findings and media reports: Consistency of themes

In concluding our review of domains of vulnerability among suburban youth, we note that the preceding suggestions stemming from nascent empirical work are entirely resonant with recent media reports on these children and their families.[53] Some of them are summarized here:

• A recent *Newsweek* story described the "insane frenzy" of multiple child activities among upper-middle-class families and linked it with a loss of the "soul of childhood and the joy of family life." Among the experts' opinions cited was this: "'These are supposed to be the years that kids wander around and pal around, without being faced with the pressures of the real world,' says Stanford's [William] Damon. Instead, he says, 'the parenting experience is being ruined and parents' effectiveness is being diminished. They're not giving the right kind of guidance, dispensing wisdom about life. It's all about how to get into Yale.'"[54]

• A *New York Times* report based on interviews with child psychotherapists indicated that many upper-class children experience high emotional distress, often a result of being overscheduled with too many organized activities: "Doctors say that some children feel so much pressure for high performance that they develop stress-related symptoms like insomnia, stomachaches, headaches, anxiety, and depression."[55]

• A story based on dozens of interviews with suburban middle school children described casual attitudes to substance use beginning as early as age thirteen. "Boys . . . casually discussed the beers they liked and joked about [the] 'international 4:20 club', which is supposed to be the universal time to smoke pot." Factors implicated include parents' demanding careers and long work hours, as well as pressures faced by the children themselves, particularly related to their future higher education: "We work so hard during the week, because of college pressure, that by the weekends we're totally, like, *Let the games begin!*"[56]

• A news report entitled "Face of Heroin: It's Younger and Suburban" indicated that the popularity of heroin has shifted from the inner city to the suburbs; the suburban youth interviewed for the story—all undergoing treatment for heroin addiction—each mentioned stress at school or home as precipitating their heroin use as teenagers.[57]

• Survey findings by the nonpartisan Urban Institute revealed that many affluent adults regularly leave their children without adult supervision after school, and that lack of after-school supervision exacerbates the risk of substance use as well as other adjustment problems.[58]

• In a PBS "Frontline" show featuring a prosperous Georgia town, parents were described as a professional group of high achievers who expected a lot of their children by way of achievement. Interviews with a cross-section of youth revealed sexual promiscuity and substance use among children as young as twelve, and a strong "desire for attention—even discipline—from parents." Developmental experts, reacting to this show, commented: "What is [particularly] disturbing . . . is the tremendous disconnect that exists between the children of Rockdale County and their families" (Robert Blum). "Between the hours of 3:00 P.M. and 7:00 P.M. on weekdays . . . many adolescents have left the supervision of the school setting where they do not report to anyone as their parents finish their workday" (Richard Gallagher).

"We heard a lot about emptiness. Houses that were empty and devoid of supervision, adult presence, oversight. There was for far too many of the adolescents a fundamental emptiness of purpose; a sense that they were not needed, not connected to adults, to tasks, to anything meaningful other than the raw and relentless pursuit of pleasure" (Michael Resnick).[59]

Conclusion

Children living in affluent, upwardly mobile families are typically thought of as being at low psychosocial risk, but accumulating research suggests that they cannot be assumed to be psychologically healthy. In fact, many of these youngsters may experience nontrivial levels of stressors that are unique to communities such as theirs; they may experience considerable emotional distress and engage in high substance use. To be sure, some will argue that problems of these youth should not be of concern to applied developmental scientists, because their parents can secure ample help for them (as in the form of psychotherapy).

Even as such arguments are weighed, it must be acknowledged that many parents do not seek help for their children despite awareness that they are troubled,[60] and further that no child, no matter how affluent, can independently obtain ongoing treatment for himself or herself. As developmental scholars continue the much-needed attention to youth outside the mainstream majority of middle-class society, therefore, it would be wise to remain cognizant that those ostensibly most privileged can also confront substantial threats to their psychological well-being: "contextual risks" may not be unique to just one extreme on the sociodemographic continuum.

Notes

1. Garcia Coll, C., Lamberty, G., Jenkins, R., McAdoo, H. P., Crnic, K., Wasik, B. H., & Vazquez Garcia, H. (1996). An integrative model for the

study of developmental competencies in minority children. *Child Development*, 67, 1891–1914; Luthar, S. S. (1999). *Poverty and children's adjustment*. Thousand Oaks, CA: Sage.

2. Buss, D. M. (2000). The evolution of happiness. *American Psychologist*, 55, 15–23.

3. Diener, E. (2000). Subjective well being: The science of happiness and a proposal for a national index. *American Psychologist*, 55, 34–43; Meyers, D. G. (2000). The funds, friends, and faith of happy people. *American Psychologist*, 55, 56–67.

4. Meyers (2000), p. 61.

5. Brickman, P., & Campbell, D. T. (1971). Hedonic relativism and planning the good society. In M. H. Appley (Ed.), *Adaptation-level theory* (pp. 287–305). Orlando: Academic Press.

6. Diener (2000); Meyers (2000); Csikszentmihalyi, M. (1999). If we are so rich, why aren't we happy? *American Psychologist*, 54, 821–827.

7. Nesse, R. M., & Williams, G. C. (1994). *Why we get sick*. New York: New York Times Books.

8. Buss (2000).

9. Csikszentmihalyi, M. (1999), p. 823.

10. Kasser, T., & Ryan, R. M. (1996). Further examining the American dream: Differential correlates of intrinsic and extrinsic goals. *Personality and Social Psychology Bulletin, 22*, 280–287.

11. Csikszentmihalyi, M., & Schneider, B. (2000). *Becoming adult: How teenagers prepare for the world of work*. New York: Basic Books.

12. Hurley, L. P., & Lustbader, L. L. (1997). Project support: Engaging children and families in the educational process. *Adolescence, 32*, 523–531; Luthar, S. S., & D'Avanzo, K. (1999). Contextual factors in substance use: A study of suburban and inner-city adolescents. *Development and Psychopathology, 11*, 845–876.

13. U.S. Department of Health and Human Services. (1999). *America's Children*. (www.childstats.gov/ac1999.asp)

14. Johnston, L. D., O'Malley, P. M., & Bachman, J. G. (1998). *National survey results on drug use from the Monitoring the Future study (1975–1997): Vol. 1. Secondary school students* (chapters four and five). Rockville, MD: National Institute on Drug Abuse.

15. Beuhring, T., Saewyc, E. M., Stern, C. B., & Resnick, M. D. (1996). *Voice of Connecticut youth: A statewide survey of adolescent health*. University of Minnesota, Minneapolis.

16. National Institute on Drug Abuse. (2000). *Statement of the director at the U.S. Senate Caucus on the International Narcotics Control*. (www.drugabuse.gov/testimony/7-25-00Testimony.html)

17. Leshner, A. L. (2000). *Club Drugs*. (Community Alert Bulletin.) (http://165.112.78.61/ClubAlert/Clubdrugalert.html)

18. Bronfenbrenner, U. (1977). Toward an experimental ecology of human development. *American Psychologist, 32*, 513–531.

19. Sameroff, A. J., & Chandler, M. J. (1975). Reproductive risk and the continuum of caretaking casualty. In F. D. Horowitz, M. Hetherington, S. Scarr-Alaptek, & G. Siegel (Eds.), *Review of child development research* (pp. 187–243). Chicago: University of Chicago.

20. Cicchetti, D., & Lynch, M. (1993). Toward an ecological/transactional model of community violence and child maltreatment: Consequences for children's development. *Psychiatry: Interpersonal and Biological Processes, 56,* 96–118.

21. Cicchetti, D., & Schneider-Rosen, K. (1986). An organizational approach to childhood depression. In M. Rutter, C. Izard, & P. Read (Eds.), *Depression in young people, clinical and developmental perspectives* (pp. 71–134). New York: Guilford; Sroufe, L. A. (1979). The coherence of individual development: Early care attachment, and subsequent developmental issues. *American Psychologist, 34,* 834–841.

22. Luthar, S. S. (1997). Sociodemographic disadvantage and psychosocial adjustment: Perspectives from developmental psychopathology. In S. S. Luthar, J. A. Burack, D. Cicchetti, & J. R. Weisz, (Eds.) *Developmental psychopathology: Perspectives on adjustment, risk, and disorder* (pp. 459–485). New York: Cambridge.

23. Wentzel, K. R., & Caldwell, K., (1997). Friendships, peer acceptance, and group membership: Relations to academic achievement in middle school. *Child Development, 68*(6), 1198–1209.

24. Luthar & D'Avanzo (1999).

25. Ibid.

26. Ibid.

27. Ibid.

28. Way, N., Stauber, H. Y., Nakkula, M. J., & London, P. (1994). Depression and substance use in two divergent high school cultures: A quantitative and qualitative analysis. *Journal of Youth and Adolescence, 23,* 331–357.

29. Luthar & D'Avanzo (1999).

30. Ibid.

31. D'Avanzo, K., & Luthar, S. S. (2001, Apr.). *Psychopathology and competence in relation to substance use: Two-year cross-domain links among suburban youth.* Symposium conducted at the Society for Research in Child Development, Minneapolis, Minnesota.

32. Luthar & D'Avanzo (1999).

33. Luthar, S. S., & Becker, B. E. (in press). *Privileged but pressured: A study of affluent youth.* Child Development.

34. Luthar & D'Avanzo (1999).

35. Steinhausen, H., & Metzke, C. W. (1998). Frequency and correlates of substance use among preadolescents and adolescents in a Swiss epidemiological study. *Journal of Child Psychology and Psychiatry and Allied Disciplines, 39,* 387–397.

36. DeCarlo, L. T., & Luthar, S. S. (2000). Analysis and class validation of a measure of parental values perceived by preadolescents: An application of a latent class model for rankings. *Educational and Psychological Measurement, 60,* 578–591.

37. Frost, R. O., Marten, P., Lahart, C., & Rosenblate, R. (1990). The dimensions of perfectionism. *Cognitive Therapy and Research, 13,* 449–468.

38. Luthar & D'Avanzo (1999).

39. Baumrind, D. (1987). A developmental perspective on adolescent risk taking in contemporary America. In *Adolescent Social Behavior and Health,* New Directions for Child Development, 37, 93–125.

40. Hall, G. S. (1904). *Adolescence* (vols. 1 and 2). Upper Saddle River, NJ: Prentice Hall.

41. Pine, D. S., Cohen, P., Gurley, D., Brook, J., & Ma, Y. (1998). The risk for early-adulthood anxiety and depressive disorders in adolescents with anxiety and depressive disorders. *Archives of General Psychiatry, 55,* 56–64.

42. Zucker, R. A., Fitzgerald, H. E., & Moses, H. D. (1995). Emergence of alcohol problems and the several alcoholisms: A developmental perspective on etiologic theory and life course trajectory. In D. Cicchetti & D. Cohen (Eds.), *Manual of developmental psychopathology: Vol. 2. Risk, disorder, and adaptation* (pp. 677–711). New York: Wiley.

43. Chen, K., & Kandel, D. B. (1995). The natural history of drug use from adolescence to the mid thirties in a general population sample. *American Journal of Public Health, 85,* 41–47.

44. Luthar, S. S., & Burack, J. A. (2000). Adolescent wellness: In the eye of the beholder? In D. Cicchetti, J. Rappaport, I. Sandler, and R. Weissberg (Eds.), *The promotion of wellness in children and adolescents* (pp. 29–57). Washington, D.C.: Child Welfare League of America.

45. Luthar & D'Avanzo (1999).

46. Pine et al. (1998).

47. Salovey, P., Rothman, A. J., Detweiler, J. B., & Steward, W. T. (2000). Emotional states and physical health. *American Psychologist, 55,* 110–121.

48. Grant, B., & Dawson, D. A. (1997). Age at onset of alcohol use and its association with DSM-IV alcohol abuse and dependence: Results from the National Longitudinal Alcohol Epidemiologic Survey. *Journal of Substance Abuse, 9,* 103–110; Sher, K., & Gotham, H. (1999). Pathological alcohol involvement: A developmental disorder of young adulthood. In D. Cicchetti, B. Nurcombe, & S. S. Luthar (Eds.), *Development and Psychopathology: Vol. 11. Special Issue: Developmental Approaches to Substance Use and Abuse* (pp. 933–956). New York: Cambridge University Press.

49. Zucker, Fitzgerald, & Moses (1995).

50. Luthar & D'Avanzo (1999).

51. Baer, J. S., MacLean, M. G., & Marlatt, G. A. (1998). Linking etiology and treatment for adolescent substance abuse: Toward a better match. In R. Jessor (Ed.), *New perspectives on adolescent risk behavior.* New York: Cambridge University Press.

52. Sher & Gotham (1999).

53. Luthar & Becker (in press).

54. Kantrowitz, B., & Wingert, P. (2001, January 29). The parent trap. *Newsweek,* pp. 51–52.

55. Gilbert, S. (1999, August 3). For some children, it's an after-school pressure cooker. *New York Times,* p. F7.

56. Franks, L. (2000, February). The sex lives of your children. *Talk,* pp. 102–107.

57. Wren, C. S. Face of heroin: It's younger and suburban. *New York Times,* p. B5.

58. One in five children alone after school, study says. (2000, September 11). *New York Times,* p. A18.

59. For a full report on the "Frontline" show and transcripts, see www.pbs. org/wgbh/pages/frontline/shows/georgia/etc/synopsis.html.

60. Puura, K., Almqvist, F., Tamminen, T., Piha, J., Kumpulainen, K., Rasa-nen, E., Moilanen, I., & Koivisto, A. (1998). Children with symptoms of depression—What do the adults see? *Journal of Child Psychology and Psychiatry, 39*, 577–585.

SUNIYA S. LUTHAR *is professor of psychology and education at Teachers College, Columbia University.*

SHAWN J. LATENDRESSE *is a doctoral student in the Department of Human Development at Teachers College, Columbia University.*

Search Institute's integrated program of research on the linkages among community, developmental assets, and health outcomes is discussed. Recommendations are made for building a science that is dedicated to exploring pathways to developmental success.

Adolescent development in social and community context: A program of research

Peter L. Benson

IN THE LAST DECADE, Search Institute has launched a comprehensive program of theory building and research intended to understand the linkages among communities, developmental assets, and health outcomes. In this integrated stream of work, several arenas of investigation have emerged: (1) definition and measurement of developmental assets, (2) the predictive utility of developmental assets for explaining both risk behaviors and thriving behaviors, (3) the ecological and intrapersonal sources of developmental assets, (4) the nature and dynamics of an asset-building community, and (5) strategies and tactics that mobilize the asset-building capacity of a community. The primary intent is to develop an interdisciplinary, ecological, and applied line of inquiry that understands and

Note: Preparation of this chapter was supported, in part, by grants from the William T. Grant Foundation and Thrive Foundation for Youth. Further information about this research can be obtained from Peter L. Benson, Search Institute, 615 First Ave. N.E., Minneapolis, MN 55413.

NEW DIRECTIONS FOR YOUTH DEVELOPMENT, NO. 95, FALL 2002 © WILEY PERIODICALS, INC.

activates local capacity to reshape and energize the developmental infrastructure within the community.

As described in several recent publications,[1] we use two interchangeable names for this work: community-based human development and asset-based community and human development. The latter concept yokes our work directly with several leading approaches to community development: asset-based community development, with its accent on using the real but often hidden strengths of a community to lead and direct the process of change[2]; and the national healthy community movement, which accentuates citizen engagement in articulating and addressing local civic, health, economic, and ecological issues.[3]

In linking the human development and community development spheres, we draw on a number of intellectual and research traditions. The concept of community within the field of child and adolescent development owes considerable debt to Bronfenbrenner's theoretical foundations on the ecology of human development,[4] as well as to the significant work of Jessor and his colleagues on social—cultural influences on adolescent behavior.[5] This line of theory and research helped to trigger a coherent view of the child's embeddedness within a complex pattern of social institutions[6] and design of community-based interventions aimed at a range of issues, including school readiness and prevention of juvenile delinquency.[7] Lerner's work on developmental contextualization[8] has added to the understanding of community context in its articulation of the ecologies that inform development and how adolescents influence their social contexts. The implications of this work for policy and program are significant.[9]

The developmental asset framework

As studies of the processes related to resilience and of the relation between community contexts and adolescent development have accumulated, intervention and prevention efforts develop around these concepts in an attempt to alter the developmental pathways of young people. Some of these efforts have focused on risk reduction; others have focused more intentionally on promoting positive development.[10] Asset development is a relatively new conceptualization of positive human development, synthesizing contextual and individual factors that, when present, serve to protect from, or inhibit, health-compromising behavior and enhance the opportunity for positive developmental outcomes.

Structuring and measuring the developmental asset framework has four major purposes. First, it seeks to provide a language for core elements of positive human development, with emphasis on developmental processes, experiences, and resources known to promote short-term and long-term well-being. Second, it is intended to create a unified picture of positive development capable of uniting citizens and multiple socializing systems around a shared vision. In this way, it is an attempt to create a common language that has the potential of contributing to a public consensus on what "our" children and adolescents need to succeed.

Third, it seeks to empower and mobilize residents, families, neighborhoods, youth organizations, religious institutions, and the rest of the community sector to take action. Finally, through a survey and reporting process that presents a portrait of developmental assets among a community's youth, the framework and its local measurement serves as a kind of call to action to strengthen developmental processes and experiences for all youth within a community. As of mid-2002, about seven hundred U.S. communities are using the framework to organize and launch communitywide, asset-building initiatives. This national movement is organized and supported at Search Institute through its National Healthy Community–Healthy Youth Initiative.

Scientific and conceptual roots

As described in a series of publications,[11] the developmental asset framework emerged by integrating several strands of theory and research. The framework of developmental assets establishes a set of benchmarks for positive child and adolescent development, weaving together in an priori conceptual model a taxonomy of developmental targets requiring both family and community engagement to ensure their acquisition. The original configuration of thirty developmental assets was described in several publications[12] as well as in data-based reports developed for each of 460 school districts. These reports were based on Search Institute's *Profiles of Student Life: Attitudes and Behaviors*, a survey designed to measure the developmental assets. In 1996, the model was expanded to forty developmental assets, on the basis of analysis of data gathered on 254,000 students, additional synthesis of child and adolescent research, and consultation with researchers and practitioners.

The framework's intellectual foundations are rooted in empirical studies of child and adolescent development, with additional focus on the more applied literature of prevention, protective factors, and resiliency. How one captures this extensive scientific legacy in a finite number of developmental targets depends on one's definition of health outcomes. The assets initially are framed around the second decade of life, roughly spanning the middle school and high school years. The research synthesis focused on integrating developmental experiences that are widely known to inform three types of health outcome: (1) prevention of high-risk behaviors (substance use, violence, sexual intercourse, dropping out of school); (2) enhancement of thriving outcomes (school success, affirmation of diversity, a proactive approach to nutrition and exercise, and so on); and (3) resiliency, or the capacity to rebound in the face of adversity.

In further delimiting the number of potential elements, we looked for developmental factors that, when present, were particularly robust in predicting health outcomes and for which there is evidence that their predictive utility holds across sex, race-ethnicity, and family income. Finally, the assets were conceived to reflect core developmental processes. Accordingly, they include relationships, social experiences, social environments, patterns of interaction, norms, and competencies over which a community of people has considerable control. That is, the assets are more about the primary processes of socialization than the equally important arenas of economy, services, and the bricks and mortar of a city.

Asset categories

The forty developmental assets are both a theoretical framework and a research model. Because the model is also intended to have practical significance for mobilizing communities, the assets are placed in categories that have conceptual integrity and that can be described easily to the people of a community. They are grouped into twenty external assets (health-promoting features of the environment) and twenty that are internal (commitments, values, competencies, and so on). The external assets are grouped into four categories: (1) support, (2) empowerment, (3) boundaries and expectations, and (4) constructive use of time. The internal assets are placed in four categories: (1) commitment to learning, (2) positive values, (3) social competencies, and (4) positive identity. The scientific foundations for the eight categories and each of the forty assets are described in more detail in Benson[13] and Scales and Leffert.[14]

The external assets refer to the positive developmental experiences of relationship and opportunity that adults offer young people. They emerge through constant exposure to informal interactions with caring and principled adults and peers, and they are reinforced by a larger network of community institutions. The internal assets are competencies, skills, and self-perceptions that young people develop gradually over time. A community can ensure that young people have external assets, but internal ones do not simply occur; they evolve gradually as a result of numerous experiences. From a community mobilization standpoint, it is conceptually sound to organize around increasing the external assets, but the growth of internal assets is a slower, more complex, and idiosyncratic process of self-regulation.

The support assets cover a range of opportunities for experiencing affirmation, approval, and acceptance, within multiple settings (family, intergenerational relationships, neighborhood, school). These experiences include relational support and a warm and caring environment.[15]

The empowerment assets represent a constellation of factors that encourage children and adolescents to become actors within a community, with a focus on being valued and useful within it.[16] The asset of safety is seen as an important subtext for empowerment.

Early models for understanding what affects adolescent development focused on the singular effects of the family environment on child development. Recent explanations have gone beyond those models and suggested that the socialization strategies in the broader community are no less important for adolescent development.[17] As such, the boundary-and-expectation assets address the importance of a clear and consistent message in a number of contexts (including the family) in which adolescents are involved, and the presence of adults and peers who model positive and responsible behaviors.

The constructive-use-of-time assets pertains to the important array of constructive opportunities that should be available to all young people, particularly in the ten-to-eighteen range. Bronfenbrenner[18] suggested that healthy development should include a variety of such activities. Ideally, these are settings that connect youth to caring adults who hope to nurture their skills and capacities.[19] Religious institutions are one of the few remaining intergenerational communities to which youth have access. They are places of multiple generations, with people bound together, to a greater or lesser degree, through a shared perspective and shared values. The congregation as an intergenerational community, however, represents potential more than reality, because most communities of faith have become as age-segregated as is the rest of society. Nevertheless, there is an extensive scientific literature showing that religious participation broadly enhances caring for others and helps reduce multiple forms of risk-taking behavior, even after controlling for family background.[20]

The commitment-to-learning assets include a combination of personal beliefs, values, and skills known to enhance academic success.[21] They include engagement in learning activities, a sense of belonging to the school environment, the motivation to do well, and expectations for success.[22] Commitment to learning has a number of sources; parental attitudes, encouragement, involvement, and modeling are vital. The quality of schooling matters, through its formal and informal curricula. Norms that encourage high attention to educational tasks, by peer group and community, also are instrumental.

The six positive-value assets represent prosocial values and those of personal character.[23] These six reflect a significant public consensus on values, with some evidence that they approximate a universal core of values within an advanced technological society. Just as important, there is research evidence supporting the role of each in health promotion.[24]

The social-competency assets include a personal skill set needed to deal with the myriad choices, challenges, and opportunities presented in a complex society. They generally refer to adaptive functioning in which the individual may call on personal and environmental resources.[25] Social competence is thought to develop within a social context[26] and includes planning and decision-making skills, interpersonal and cultural competence, resistance skills, and the ability to resolve conflict peacefully.[27]

Identity formation is a critical task of adolescent development.[28] As such, the positive-identity assets focus on young people's views of themselves in relation to their future, self-esteem, and sense of purpose and power.[29]

Research on developmental assets

Descriptive and predictive data on developmental assets have recently been summarized by Benson.[30] The developmental assets are assessed in a 156-item survey instrument, administered anonymously in public school districts in a classroom setting guided by standardized instructions. The instrument also assesses numerous thriving indicators (for example, school success, affirmation of diversity) and risk behaviors (violence, substance use, sexual behavior, and so on). Students place completed surveys in an envelope, which is then sealed and mailed to Search Institute for processing and generation of a school district report. Typically, school districts choose to survey a complete census of all sixth to twelfth grade students attending school on the day the survey is administered.

A large and diverse sample

Since 1990, more than fifteen hundred cities have conducted this survey, many as an early step in launching a communitywide asset-building initiative. There is a significant mix of urban, suburban, and rural districts included in this ongoing survey assessment process. Our recent scientific publications use an aggregate sample of 99,462 sixth to twelfth grade youth from public alternative schools in 213 cities and towns in the United States that administered the survey during the 1996–97 academic year.

An updated and expanded sample will become the focus of a next wave of analysis, which was begun in early 2002. This sample of 217,277 sixth to twelfth grade students aggregates across 318 communities. All data were collected in the 1999–2000 school year. Using U.S. census figures, data have been weighted on urban or nonurban setting and race or ethnicity. A preliminary comparison of the older and newer samples suggests only minor and largely nonmeaningful changes in asset profile.

The survey is primarily used as a means of communicating aggregate data on a community's youth. A report, developed for each city or school district that uses the survey, often becomes a widely shared document and is used to frame communitywide discussion and serves as a focal point for mobilization around raising healthy youth.[31] A dichotomous form of reporting the assets, whereby each asset is simplified into a single percentage of youth who have, or do not have, each asset, is used as an effective method for communicating the asset profile to diverse community audiences. This also permits simple summation of the average number of youth assets in any given community.

Survey results

A growing body of publications describe the psychometric properties of the survey instrument,[32] demographic differences in asset profile,[33] and the predictive utility of the asset framework for explaining both risk and thriving behaviors.[34]

Two themes dominate these studies. First is the consistent finding that most adolescents show only a minority of the developmental assets. The mean number of assets is 19.3, on a scale comprising forty binary variables. More than half (56 percent) of the newer aggregated sample evince twenty or fewer developmental assets. When the sample is broken into four asset levels, we find that 15 percent possess a total number of assets of ten or fewer, 41 percent possess eleven to twenty, 35 percent have twenty-one to thirty, and 9 percent attain thirty or more.

Diminishing assets

By grade, the mean decreases from 23.1 in grade six to 18.3 in grade twelve. Boys average about three assets fewer than girls (17.8 and 20.7, respectively). A particularly important finding is that the mean number of assets is relatively similar when comparing students in communities of varying size (from ten thousand to a quarter million or more). Variation across communities is less than expected and reinforces the idea that every community has a significant proportion of adolescents who lack key developmental building blocks in their lives. It should be noted here that these findings are based on youth who attended American middle schools and high schools. If out-of-school twelve-to-eighteen-year-olds were also captured in this assessment, the reported percentages would likely be lower.

Family income is not measured in the survey. However, in a study done in Minneapolis, we looked at how the developmental assets vary as a function of the city's eleven planning districts, which differ substantially in average family income, property values, and resources. Across these eleven geographical areas of the city, the average number from among the forty assets ranged from 16.7 to 20.1.[35] Not surprisingly, as average wealth rises, assets rise. But to put this in context, note that the difference is only about three developmental assets when comparing the least and most affluent planning districts.

In all demographic categories, certain asset groups are particularly fragile. Among these are many of the specific assets in the support, engagement, boundary–and–expectation, and social-competency categories. Total sample and subgroup percentages for each of forty assets are reported in a number of publications.[36]

The power of multiple assets

The second theme has to do with the cumulative or additive nature of the developmental assets in explaining risk and thriving behavior. That is, as assets rise in number, we see a profound reduction in each of nine risk behavior patterns (alcohol use, tobacco use, illicit drug use, antisocial behavior, violence, school failure, sexual activity, attempted suicide, and gambling). The cumulative effect is equally powerful in predicting thriving behaviors, with an increase in assets associated with a dramatic rise in academic achievement, school grades, leadership, prosocial behavior, delay of gratification, and affirmation of diversity. Many of our studies pinpoint subsets of assets that are particularly germane to a risk or thriving behavior, but addressing a more comprehensive vision of child and adolescent health (that is, protection from many types of risk behavior and the pursuit of many forms of thriving) requires attention to the full complement of developmental assets.

More sophisticated analysis documents the relative power of the asset framework. Regression analyses are used to assess the extent to which the developmental assets are useful in predicting either a reduction in risk behaviors or a promotion of thriving indicators. Those analyses have shown that demographic variables accounted for a range of 5–14 percent of the total variance of each model constructed to examine risk behavior. In each analysis, the developmental assets contributed a significant amount over and above the influence of demographic variables, accounting for 16–35 percent of the variance explained in the reduction of each individual risk behavior pattern and for 57 percent of the variance in a composite index of them. The total regression model (assets with demographics) explained 66 percent of the variance in this composite index.

"Problem-free is not fully prepared"

Adolescent health is often understood as the absence of symptom, pathology, or health-compromising behavior. This incomplete view of well-being, of course, mimics the "medical model" approach to health. The emerging field of youth development places particular emphasis on expanding the concept of health to include the kind of skills, behaviors, and competencies needed to succeed in employment, education, and civic life. A common mantra in youth development circles is that "problem-free is not fully prepared."[37]

The concept of thriving indicators has been posited to reflect this domain of positive outcomes.[38] Multiple thriving behavior measures are embedded in the developmental asset survey instrument. Regression analyses show that the developmental asset framework is also a powerful prediction of thriving measures taken one at a time or in combination. Across each of six racial or ethnic groups (African American, Asian American, Hispanic and Latino, Native American, multiracial, white), developmental assets explained 47–54 percent of the variance in a composite thriving index (prosocial behavior, leadership, affirmation of diversity) over and above demographic variables.[39]

Of particular import is the role of developmental assets in academic achievement. Students who report a high number of assets (thirty-one to forty) are 2.5 times more likely (53 percent versus 19 percent) to report "getting mostly A's" in school compared to students with eleven to twenty assets and about 8 times more likely than those reporting ten or fewer assets (7 percent).[40] A recent study in a midwestern city allows us to merge individual asset profiles with school records. We find that developmental assets are strongly linked to grade point average and to actual grades in English, science, and mathematics.[41] Other research is under way that links developmental assets with archival data on state benchmark tests.

The observation that assets have a cumulative or pile-up effect adds to an emerging literature on this phenomenon. Heretofore, most of this research has focused on the pile-up effect of risk indicators on problem behavior. One exception to this, and consonant with the cumulative impact of developmental assets, is Jessor's work on the additive nature of protective factors in reducing several forms of risk taking.[42]

The sources of developmental assets

Built into the design of the developmental asset framework are a series of external, or ecological, assets. They are organized into the domains of support, empowerment, boundaries and expectations, and structured time use. The generators of these strengths are, of course, many and varied.

Each potential asset-building resource available to a child or adolescent can be examined from several vantage points.[43] Such resources—whether family, school, peer, playground, or program—can directly influence one or more developmental strengths (support, boundaries, values, and so on). They also have the potential to serve a bridging or linking role to other developmental resources, as when a neighborhood builds connections across families or schools to connect youth to an after-school program. This linking role is akin to the concept of the mesosystem.[44] In turn, developmental settings are also dependent variables, being shaped and informed both by other proximal contexts (say, the impact of crime rates on neighborhood cohesion) and interventions (policy, a public education campaign, community education, a reform movement, social services) intended to increase the capacity of developmental settings.

Family has surely been the most studied socialization system and presents a useful prototype for understanding these multiple strength-building capacities. Lerner, Fisher, and Weinberg[45] present a particularly compelling family ecology model, linking the nurturance and socialization capacity of the family to the concept of civil society. It describes two core strategies needed to enhance these family capacities: public policy framed to build family strengths and resulting programs made accessible and available on a national scale.

In their study of adolescent success in urban families, Furstenberg and colleagues[46] focus on two complementary processes found in the success-promoting family. One is the internal life of the family and how parents or guardians deliver nurturance, support, and discipline. The second is a linking process, including how the family manages opportunity and risk in other developmental ecologies and the degree to which the parents model civic engagement.

Several recent syntheses of the family literature offer an in-depth account of family and parenting influence on a range of developmental strengths.[47] Other work draws our attention to a new generation of parenting research, aided by advances in theory, design, and analytical procedures. In essence, the search for "broad, general, main effects" in environmental influences such as parenting is giving way to "statistical interactions and moderator effects".[48] Hence, family—like any socializing system—does its work and has its effect within a dynamic of networks and webs. Though this makes isolation of specific sector effects elusive, it fuels advances in conceptualizing and studying the multiple and interconnected systems and sectors that shape and are shaped by children and adolescents.

In recent years, it has appeared that schools exist for one and only one reason: to advance achievement test scores. Learning and achievement may be the core mission, but schools have the additional capacities and accountabilities too often lost in the recent escalation of testing as a national priority. Schools, like families and neighborhoods, are also an instrument of socialization. Hence, they are a potential generator of the kind of developmental strength needed to maintain or advance societal well-being.

We choose here to make three points about the role of the school in generating developmental strengths. First, a school possesses an array of resources that can be directly brought to bear on development. One particularly cogent, recent conceptualization shows how school-level policy, climate, resource allocation, norms, training and leadership, classroom-level teaching, time management, and curriculum can be mobilized and aligned to address nearly all the developmental strengths enumerated in the first part of this chapter.[49]

The second point has to do with the powerful linking capacity of the school. In theory, a school is at the hub of a wheel, with spokes to family, neighborhood, employer, youth organization, and social service delivery system. The lines of potential influence, of course, go two ways: schools can help to mobilize the strength-building capacity of these constituencies and draw them into learning and human developmental partnerships.

Finally, academic achievement is strongly informed by a child's developmental strengths. A new line of inquiry connecting developmental assets to educational outcomes is emerging.[50] Initial results, reviewed in depth earlier in this chapter, suggest two major conclusions: first, the higher the total number of developmental assets, the stronger a variety of educational attainment outcomes, including class rank and grade point average in core subjects; and second, the total number of assets as well as a particular configuration of assets account for as much variance (or more) in educational achievement as do conventional schooling factors such as per-pupil expenditures, curricular requirements, teacher preparation, and leadership. As noted earlier, assets play a similar role in lessening the rate of school dropout.[51]

Though research on families and schools dominates the so-called socialization literature, there are other significant contexts of development that can, depending on their quality, developmental attentiveness, and connectedness with other community sectors, become part of the formula for building developmental assets. Four contexts have particular potential to play an additive role in building developmental strengths or a compensator role if other sectors are absent, incomplete, or dysfunctional. They are neighborhood, national and local youth organizations, faith community, and primary support (a sector to be defined in a moment).

New lines of inquiry are shedding light on these four contexts. The neighborhood is currently being studied through two lenses. In a series of studies about social control and crime in Chicago neighborhoods, Sampson and his colleagues[52] suggest that the level of social cohesion among neighbors, combined with the level of shared commitment to take action when an understanding of the common good is threatened, is strongly linked to the rate of violence, beyond what is accounted for by demographic factors such as income and residential stability. What is particularly germane here is that the definition of the common good—the glue uniting the neighborhood in shared purpose and action—typically has to do with the welfare of neighborhood children.

A relatively high percentage of American youth connect locally with such national youth-serving organizations as YMCA, YWCA, Camp Fire Boys and Girls, Boys and Girls Clubs of American, and 4-H; or with a range of other structured voluntary activities that tend to evolve at the community level.[53] The term *primary supports* has been used in a series of studies to cover the territory of before-and-after-school programs; sports teams and athletic activities; programs dedicated to dance, drama, music, and the visual arts; and libraries, museums, parks, and community centers.[54] This is a potentially rich area of developmental influence, though studies of its role in human development lags behind the social need to build or expand this sector in light of dramatic changes in other contexts of youth's lives (family, neighborhood, and so on).

Faith communities

Faith communities are too rarely on the social science radar screen. For the roughly one-half of American youth who connect to mosque, synagogue, parish, congregation, or spiritual place, developmental resources within these contexts can be brought to bear on developmental strengths. There is an historic academic interest, though certainly not in mainstream academe, in religion operationalized as both independent and dependent variables. However, when the object of inquiry is the source of young people's support, adult connection, engagement, boundary, structure, skill, and identity, these settings become as germane to the inquiry as any other. Indeed, an emerging line of study reveals important links between adolescent religious affiliation and indicators of positive development.[55] Wagener and colleagues[56] advance this line of inquiry by proposing, testing, and confirming the hypothesis that developmental assets mediate the relationship of religious influences for both risk and thriving indicators. That is, religious communities appear, in a general sense, to increase participants' access to some of the developmental strengths known to inform health outcomes.

Other contexts that could be a "delivery system" for developmental strengths are not as well studied. They include places of employment, public spaces (parks and shopping malls), and community-based rituals and ceremonies celebrating children, youth, and families. Increasingly, the role of media in its many and varied forms must be factored into any conceptual model of the contextual forces that advance (or limit) developmental strengths.

Asset-building communities

An asset-building community is a geography of place that maximizes attentiveness to promoting developmental strengths for all children and adolescents.[57] The dynamics and processes by which a community mobilizes its asset-building capacity is a relatively unexplored line of inquiry, both theoretically and empirically. An initial framework for understanding the asset-building capacity of a community offers a set of core principles.[58] Among these are the developmental redundancy (exposure to asset-building people and environments within multiple contexts), developmental depth (a focus on nurturing most or all assets in children and adolescents), and developmental breadth (extending, by purpose and design, the reach of asset-building energy to all children and adolescents).

Five sources of asset-building potential are hypothesized to exist in every community, each of which can be marshaled by way of a multiplicity of community mobilization strategies: (1) sustained relationships with adults, both within and beyond family; (2) peer group influence (when peers choose to activate their asset-building capacity); (3) socializing systems; (4) community-level social norms, ceremony, ritual, policy, and resource allocation; and (5) programs, including school-based and community-based efforts to nurture and build skills and competencies.

In this model, sources one, two, three, and five have *direct* impact on the development of youth. A common thread across them is the primacy of relationships in positive child and adolescent development. Activating all four of these energy systems—yoked together in a shared and common purpose to build developmental strengths—is a necessary process for attaining breadth, depth, and redundancy.

Within the context of American society, this vision requires considerable transformation in prevailing resident and socialization systems, norms, and operating principles. As argued in numerous publications defining this conceptual model of asset-building community,[59] American cities are typically marked by age segregation, civic disengagement, social mistrust, a loss of personal and collective efficacy, and lack of collaboration across systems.

The study of change

Marshaling community capacity to consistently and deeply attend to development of children and adolescents is conceived less as implementing a program and more as awakening latent human and institutional potential to build developmental strengths. A series of practical tools targeted to community residents and civic leaders extends conceptual and strategic counsel for mobilizing asset-building capacity. The first asset-building initiative began in St. Louis Park, Minnesota, in 1995. In the ensuing seven years, more than seven hundred other American communities began to craft communitywide initiatives. Organized as a social movement, the community is encouraged to tailor its initiatives to local reality and capacity and in response to the data from local asset profiles. Because these initiatives are complex, multisector experiments in changing local culture, and because they occur in a variety of rural, suburban, and urban settings, there is increasing investment in learning from these communities about innovation and effective practices in mobilizing residents and systems, with a feedback loop emerging to inform both the theory of community change and the development of practical resources. Several longitudinal studies under way in Colorado and Minnesota will add additional insight to this evolving knowledge about the influence of community on human development. A rigorous case study approach to studying community change is in progress.

How does change occur?

The study of how change occurs in a developmental ecology is, in actuality, an incomplete science. Much more intellectual and research energy has been invested in naming developmental nutrients and demonstrating their role in youth outcomes than in studying the complex array of strategies and procedures for moving the developmental needle forward.

A science of change and change making in service of advancing access to developmental nutrients and assets should be directed to the study of five pathways and interactions[60]:

1. Pathways to adult engagement (how to mobilize adults, both within a community and as a national force engaging in asset-building action)
2. Pathways to adolescent engagement (how to mobilize adolescents to become proactive in their own developmental journey and to activate their asset-building capacity with peers and younger children)
3. Pathways to sector transformation (how to increase delivery of developmental nutrients by way of extant socializing systems, including the family, neighborhood, congregation, school, youth organization, and place of work)
4. Pathways to community change (how to orchestrate and sustain transformation and engagement within and across multiple actors, settings, and ecologies)
5. Pathways to social change (how to promote developmentally attentive and asset-enhancing social norms, national policy, local policy, and media influence)

In building a science of pathways to change, we would be well served to look at and learn from scholarship devoted to promoting change in other arenas, among which are organizational development, economic policy, economic development, and marketing.

Igniting adult engagement in the lives of children and adolescents requires more than changing the valence of adult sentiments. Also needed is attention to giving the public skill, practice, and social norms that demand and expect constructive engagement. Recent research on social norms suggests a variety of strategies for norm change.[61]

A recent review of the community development field suggests a rich legacy of research for understanding a range of dynamics ultimately germane to building a developmentally attentive community.[62] Among them are dynamics for promoting common good ideals, citizen engagement, collective efficacy, social trust, and social capital.

Scientific exploration of a strength-based paradigm requires a deeply interdisciplinary approach, integrating at a minimum the fields of anthropology, sociology, and economics with psychology to understand and mobilize a full arsenal of ritual, social norms, and system and individual capacities necessary to the complicated but essential task of becoming a developmentally attentive community.[63] If indeed community is an important context for "production" of developmental strength, our methods of learning and discovery require approaches currently too underused and undervalued. To a considerable extent, knowledge about crucial asset-building dynamics such as intergenerational community, sustained connection with elders (of all sorts), and rituals for moving from adolescence to adulthood are vested in nonexperts—in communities organized around race, ethnicity, or worldview. Tapping this wisdom requires a significant shift in how the academy typically works, requiring instead a knowledge-generation process that brings community residents and scholars together in pursuing and producing knowledge.[64]

Producing an interdisciplinary knowledge grounded in the inherent capacity of community also requires a long-term investment in discovering the nature and sequencing of community change. This kind of comprehensive, collaborative, citizen-engaged approach also requires a patient evaluation system.[65] The American way, when it comes to evaluation, is at best an impatient system. We would argue that the demand by government agencies and foundations to show impact after a relatively short period of time fuels quick programmatic solutions and diminishes inquiry into the complex, long-term and invigorating exploration of how this culture and its communities can and must reimagine the norms, rituals, ceremonies, relationships, environments, and policies needed to grow healthy, competent, whole, and caring human beings.

Notes

1. Benson, P. L. (2002a). Developmental assets and asset-building community: Conceptual and empirical foundations. In R. M. Lerner & P. L. Benson (Eds.), *Developmental assets and asset-building communities: Implications for research, policy and practice.* Norwell, MA: Kluwer; Benson, P. L. (2002b). Toward asset-building communities: How does change occur? In Lerner & Benson; Benson, P. L., Scales, P. C., & Mannes, M. (2002). Developmental strengths and their sources: Implications for the study and practice of community-building. In R. M. Lerner, F. Jacobs, & D. Wertlieb (Eds.), *Promoting positive child, adolescent, and family development: A handbook of program and policy innovations.* Thousand Oaks, CA: Sage; Mannes, M., Benson, P. L., Kretzmann, J., & Norris, T. (2002). The American tradition of community development: implications for guiding community engagement in youth development. In Lerner, Jacobs, & Wertlieb.

2. Kretzmann, J. P., & McKnight, J. L. (1993). *Building communities from the inside out: A path toward finding and mobilizing a community's assets.* Evanston, IL: Center for Urban Affairs and Policy Research.

3. Norris, T., Ayre, D., & Clough, G. (2000). *Facilitating community change.* San Francisco: Grove Consultants International.

4. Bronfenbrenner, U. (1979). *The ecology of human development: Experiments by nature and design.* Cambridge, MA: Harvard University Press.

5. Jessor, R. (1993). Successful adolescent development among youth in high-risk settings. *American Psychologist, 48,* 117–126; Jessor, R., Graves, T. D., Hanson, R. C., & Jessor, S. L. (1968). *Society, personality, and deviant behavior: A study of a tri-ethnic community.* New York: Holt, Rinehart & Winston; Jessor, R., & Jessor, S. L. (1977). *Problem behavior and psychosocial development: A longitudinal study of youth.* Orlando: Academic Press.

6. Belsky, J. (1981). Early human experiences: A family perspective. *Developmental Psychology, 17,* 3–23; Zigler, E. (1990). Preface. In S. J. Meisels & J. P. Skonkoff (Eds.), *Handbook of early childhood intervention* (pp. ix–xiv). New York: Cambridge University Press.

7. Zigler, E., Taussig, C., & Black, K. (1992). Early childhood intervention: A promising preventative for juvenile delinquency. *American Psychologist, 47,* 997–1006.

8. Lerner, R. M. (1986). *Concepts and themes of human development* (2nd ed.). New York: Random House; Lerner, R. M. (1992). Dialectics, developmental contextualism, and further enhancement of theory about puberty and psychosocial development. *Journal of Early Adolescence, 12,* 366–388.

9. Lerner, R. M. (1995). *America's youth in crisis: challenges and options for programs and policies.* Thousand Oaks, CA: Sage.

10. Hawkins, J. D. (1992). *Communities that care: Action for drug abuse prevention.* San Francisco: Jossey-Bass; Kazdin, A. E. (1993). Adolescent mental health. *American Psychologist, 48,* 197–141; Masten, A. S., & Coatsworth, J. D. (1998). The development of competence in favorable and unfavorable environments: Lessons from research on successful children. *American Psychologist, 53,* 205–220.

11. Benson, P. L., Leffert, N., Scales, P. C., & Blyth, D. A. (1998). Beyond the "village" rhetoric: Creating healthy communities for children and adolescents. *Applied Developmental Science, 2,* 138–159.

12. Leffert, N., Benson, P. L., Scales, P. C., Sharma, A. R., Drake, D. R., & Blyth, D. A. (1998). Developmental assets: Measurement and predication of risk behaviors among adolescents. *Applied Developmental Science, 2,* 209–230; Scales, P. C., Benson, P. L., Leffert, N., & Blyth, D. A. (2000). Contribution of developmental assets to the prediction of thriving among adolescents. *Applied Developmental Science, 4*(1), 27–46.

12. Benson, P. L. (1990) *The troubled journey: A portrait of 6th-12th grade youth.* Minneapolis: Search Institute; Benson, P. L. (1996). *Developmental assets among Minneapolis youth: The urgency of promoting healthy community.* Minneapolis: Search Institute; Benson, P. L., Espeland, P., & Galbraith, J. (1994). *What kids need to succeed.* Minneapolis: Free Spirit.

13. Benson, P. L. (1997). *All kids are our kids: What communities must do to raise caring and responsible children and adolescents.* San Francisco: Jossey-Bass.

14. Scales, P. C., & Leffert, N. (1999). *Developmental assets: A synthesis of the scientific research on adolescent development.* Minneapolis: Search Institute.

15. Scales, P. C., & Gibbons, J. L. (1996). Extended family members and unrelated adults in the lives of young adolescents: A research agenda. *Journal of Early Adolescence, 16,* 365–389; Zimmerman, M. A., & Arunkumar, R. (1994). Resiliency research: Implications for schools and policy. *Social Policy Report, 8,* 1–18.

16. Zeldin, S., & Price, L. A. (1995). Creating supportive communities for adolescent development: Challenges to scholars—An introduction. *Journal of Adolescent Research, 10,* 6–14.

17. Furstenberg, F. (1993). How families manage risk and opportunity in dangerous neighborhoods. In W. J. Wilson (Ed.), *Sociology and the public agenda* (pp. 231–258). Thousand Oaks, CA: Sage; Sampson, R. J. (1997). Collective regulation of adolescent misbehavior: Validation results from eighty Chicago neighborhoods. *Journal of Adolescent Research, 12,* 227–244.

18. Bronfenbrenner (1979).

19. Blyth, D. A., & Leffert, N. (1995). Communities as contexts for adolescent development: An empirical analysis. *Journal of Adolescent Research, 100,* 64–87; Carnegie Council on Adolescent Development. (1992). *A matter of*

time: Risk and opportunity in the nonschool hours. Recommendations for strengthening community programs for youth. Washington, D.C.: Author; Dubas, J. S., & Snider, B. A. (1993). The role of community-based youth groups in enhancing learning and achievement through nonformal education. In R. M. Lerner (Ed.), *Early adolescence: Perspectives on research, policy, and intervention.* Mahwah, NJ: Erlbaum.

20. Donahue, M. J., & Benson, P. L. (1995). Religion and the well-being of adolescents. *Journal of Social Issues, 51,* 145–160.

21. Leffert et al. (2002).

22. Eccles, J. S., & Midgley, C. (1990). Changes in academic motivation and self-perception during adolescence. In R. Montemayor, G. R. Adams, & T. P. Gullotta (Eds.), *From childhood to adolescence; A transitional period? Advances in adolescent development* (Vol. 2, pp. 134–155). Thousand Oaks, CA: Sage; Wentzel, K. R. (1993). Motivation and achievement in early adolescence: The role of multiple classroom goals. *Journal of Early Adolescence, 13,* 4–20.

23. Brooks-Gunn, J., & Paikoff, R. L. (1993). "Sex is a gamble, kissing is a game": Adolescent sexuality and health promotion. In S. G. Millstein, A. C. Petersen, & E. O. Nightingale (Eds.), *Promoting the health of adolescents: New directions for the twenty-first century* (pp. 180–208). New York: Oxford University Press; Chase-Lansdale, P. L., Wakschlag, L. S., & Brooks-Gunn, J. (1995). A psychological perspective on the development of caring in children and youth: The role of the family. *Journal of Adolescence, 18,* 515–556; Eisenberg, N., Miller, P. A., Shell, R., & McNalley, S. (1991). Prosocial development in adolescence: A longitudinal study. *Development Psychology, 27,* 849–857.

24. Leffert et al. (2002).

25. Peterson, G. W., & Leigh, F. K. (1990). The family and social competence in adolescence. In T. P. Gullotta, G. R. Adams, & R. Montemayor (Eds.), *Developing social competency in adolescence. Advances in adolescent development* (Vol. 3, pp. 97–138). Thousand Oaks, CA: Sage; Waters, E., & Sroufe, L. A. (1983). Social competence as a developmental construct. *Developmental Review, 3,* 79–97.

26. Lerner, R. M. (1987). A life-span perspective for early adolescence. In R. M. Lerner & T. T. Foch (Eds.), *Biological-psychological interactions in early adolescence* (pp. 9–34). Mahwah, NJ: Erlbaum.

27. DuBois, D. L., & Hirsch, B. J. (1990). School and neighborhood friendship patterns in blacks and whites in early adolescence. *Child Development, 61,* 524–536; Mann, L., Harmoni, R., & Power, C. N. (1989). Adolescent decision making: The development of competence. *Journal of Adolescence, 12,* 265–278; Zimmerman, R. S., Sprecher, S., Langer, L. M., & Holloway, C. D. (1993). Adolescents' perceived ability to say "no" to unwanted sex. *Journal of Adolescent Research, 10,* 383–399.

28. Erikson, E. H. (1968). *Identity: Youth and crisis.* New York: Norton.

29. Diener, C. I., & Dweck, C. S. (1980). An analysis of learned helplessness: II. The Processing of success. *Journal of Personality and Social Psychology, 39,* 940–952; Garmezy, N. (1993). Children in poverty: Resilience despite risk. *Psychiatry, 56,* 127–136; Garmezy, N. (1993). Stress-resistant children: The search

for protective factors. In J. E. Stevenson (Ed.), *Journal of Child Psychology and Psychiatry, Book Supplement no. 4: Recent research in developmental psychopathology* (pp. 213–233). Oxford: Pergamon; Harter, S. (1990). Processes underlying adolescent self-concept formation. In R. Montemayor, G. R. Adams, & T. P. Gullotta (Eds.), *From childhood to adolescence: A transitional period? Advances in adolescent development* (vol. 2, pp. 205–239). Thousand Oaks, CA: Sage.

30. Benson (2002b).

31. Benson, P. L., Galbraith, J., & Espeland, P. (1998). *What teens need to succeed: Proven, practical ways to shape your own future.* Minneapolis: Free Spirit.

32. Benson (1997); Benson, Leffert, Scales, & Blyth (1998); Leffert et al. (1998); Scales, Benson, Leffert, & Blyth (2000).

33. Benson (1990); Benson (1996); Benson, P. L., Scales, P. C., Leffert, N., & Roehlkepartain, E. R. (1999). *A fragile foundation: The state of developmental assets among American youth.* Minneapolis: Search Institute; Benson, P. L., & Leffert, N. (2001). Developmental assets in childhood and adolescence. In N. J. Smelser & P. G. Baltes (Eds.), *International encyclopedia of the social and behavioral sciences.* Oxford: Elsevier; Leffert et al. (1998).

34. Benson (1997); Benson & Leffert (2001); Leffert et al. (1998); Scales, Benson, Leffert, & Blyth (2000).

35. Benson (1996).

36. Benson & Leffert (2001).

37. Pittman, K., Irby, M., & Ferber, T. (2001). Unfinished business: Further reflections on a decade of promoting youth development. In P. Benson & K. Pittman (Eds.), *Trends in youth development: Visions, realities, and challenges* (pp. 3–50). Boston: Kluwer.

38. Benson (1997); Scales, Benson, Leffert, & Blyth (2000).

39. Scales, Benson, Leffert, & Blyth (2000).

40. Benson & Leffert (2001).

41. Leffert, N., Scales, P. C., Vraa, R., Libbey, H., & Benson, P. L. (2001, under review). *The impact of developmental assets on adolescents' academic achievement.* Minneapolis: Search Institute.

42. Jessor (1993); Jessor, R., Van Den Bos, J., Vanderryn, J., Costa, F. M., & Turbin, M. S. (1995). Protective factors in adolescent problem behavior: Moderator effects and developmental change. *Developmental Psychology, 31,* 923–933.

43. Benson, Scales, & Mannes (2002).

44. Bronfenbrenner (1979).

45. Lerner, R. M., Fisher, C. B., & Weinberg, R. A. (2000). Toward a science for the people: Promoting civil society through the application of developmental science. *Child Development, 71*(1), 11–20.

46. Furstenberg, F. F., Cook, T. D., Eccles, J., Elder, G. H., & Sameroff, A. (1999). *Managing to make it: Urban families and adolescent success.* Chicago: University of Chicago Press.

47. Leffert et al. (2002); Sampson, R. J. (2001). How do communities undergird or undermine human development: Relevant contexts and social mechanisms. In A. Booth & A. C. Crouter (Eds.), *Does it take a village? Community effects on children, adolescents and families.* Mahwah, NJ: Erlbaum.

48. Collins, W. A., Maccoby, E. E., Steinberg, Hetherington, E. M., & Borenstein, M. H. (2000). Contemporary research on parenting: The case for nature and nurture. *American Psychologist, 55,* 218–232.

49. Starkman, N., Scales, P. C., & Roberts, C. (1999). *Great places to learn: How asset-building schools help students succeed.* Minneapolis: Search Institute.

50. Scales, P. C., & Taccogna, J. (2000). Caring to try: How building students' developmental assets can promote school engagement and success. *NASSP Bulletin, 84,* 69–78; Scales, Benson, Leffert, & Blyth (2000); Scales, P. C., Blyth, D. A., Berkas, T. H., & Kielsmeier, J. C. (2000). The effects of service-learning on middle school students' social responsibility and academic success. *Journal of Early Adolescence, 20,* 332–358; Starkman, Scales, & Roberts (1999).

51. Leffert et al. (1998).

52. Sampson, R. J., Raudenbush, S. W., & Earls, F. (1997). Neighborhoods and violent crime: A multi-level study of collective efficacy. *Science, 277*(5328), 918–924; Sampson, R. J., Morenoff, J. D., & Earls, F. (1999). Beyond social capital: Spatial dynamics of collective efficacy for children. *American Sociological Review, 64,* 633–660.

53. Larson, R. W. (2000). Toward a psychology of positive youth development. *American Psychologist, 55,* 170–183.

54. Wynn, J. (1997). *Primary supports, schools, and other sects: Implications for learning and civic life.* (Paper prepared for Harvard Project on Schooling and Children.) Chicago: Chapin Hall Center for Children, University of Chicago.

55. Paragment, K. I., & Park, C. L. (1995). Merely a defense? The variety of religious means and ends. *Journal of Social Issues, 51*(2), 13–32; Resnick, M. D., Bearman, P. S., Blum, R. W., Bauman, K. E., Harris, K. M., Jones, J., Tabor, J., Beeuhring, T., Sieving, R. E., Shew, M., Ireland, M., Bearinger, L. H., & Udry, J. R. (1997). Protecting adolescents from harm: Findings from the National Longitudinal Study on Adolescent Health. *Journal of the American Medical Association, 278*(10), 823–832; Werner, E., & Smith, R. (1992). *Overcoming the odds: High-risk children from birth to adulthood.* New York: Cornell University Press; Youniss, J., McLellan, J. A., & Yates, M. (1999). Religion, community service, and identity in American youth. *Journal of Adolescence, 22,* 243–253.

56. Wagener, L. M., Furrow, J. L., King, P. E., Leffert, N., & Benson, P. L. (in press). Religion and developmental resources. *Review of Religious Research.*

57. Benson (1997).

58. Ibid.; Benson, Leffert, Scales, & Blyth (1998).

59. Benson, Leffert, Scales, & Blyth (1998).

60. Benson (2002a).

61. Scales, P. C., Benson, P. L., Roehlkepartain, E. C., Hintz, N. R., Sullivan, T. K., Mannes, M., & Grothe, R. (2001). The role of neighborhood and community in building developmental assets for children and youth: a national study of social norms among American adults. *Journal of Community Psychology, 29*(6), 703–727.

62. Mannes, Benson, Kretzmann, & Norris (2002).
63. Benson (2002b).
64. Furstenberg et al. (1999).
65. Benson (2002a).

PETER L. BENSON *is president of Search Institute, in Minneapolis.*

This chapter describes a framework for conceptualizing interventions intended to create the conditions linked to positive youth development. These interventions involve strategies designed to enhance either the will or the capacity of individuals, organizations, systems, or communities to change.

7

Creating the conditions linked to positive youth development

Robert C. Granger

THIS VOLUME ILLUSTRATES several noteworthy points of agreement among scholars interested in theory and practice regarding successful youth development. This consensus includes the usefulness of developmental system theories, the premium they place on emphasizing and understanding the transactions among developing youth and their ecologies, the intellectual and analytical power gained by considering youth's strengths and assets, and the realization that we have much to learn about the occurrence of all of this in various cultural contexts. There is also an explicit acknowledgment in several of the chapters that we know better how to describe the trajectory of youth development than how to intentionally help youth succeed. This chapter reviews this consensus, suggests that a first-order intellectual question concerns creating the conditions

Note: Further information about this research can be obtained from Robert C. Granger, William T. Grant Foundation, 570 Lexington Ave., 18th Floor, New York, NY 10022.

NEW DIRECTIONS FOR YOUTH DEVELOPMENT, NO. 95, FALL 2002 © WILEY PERIODICALS, INC.

linked to successful development, and explores a framework for conceptualizing such interventions.

A convergence of theory, empirical studies, and practice

Prior to the 1960s, most developmental theorists assumed that an individual's developmental potential and patterns were largely set at birth and that the role of the "environment" (including attempts to modify the environment via social policies and other means) was to support the unfolding of genetic endowment. But early studies of environmental influences[1] dramatically suggested the power of the environment, while the seminal writings of J. McVicker Hunt,[2] Piaget,[3] Bronfenbrenner,[4] and others focused theory and practice on the transactions between and among the developing child and the surrounding ecologies. This volume rests in that tradition.

Configuring relationships and developmental contexts

Moving beyond debate about the relative contribution of various factors that shape development (nature-nurture, the importance of family and peers), developmental system theorists[5] stress that development occurs in a set of relations among "the multiple levels of organization that comprise the substance of human life."[6] One implication of this systems approach is that no particular interaction, context, or moment is all important.[7] Rather, what is important is the configuration of these relationships over time, setting, and developmental stage. Inexorably, this formulation of development draws scholars and persons interested in improving developmental opportunity toward this configuration. How can it be productively changed by policy, education, or other means?

Strengths and assets

As Lerner and colleagues observe (in this volume), a powerful adjunct to developmental systems theory is a focus on the strengths and assets that constitute and are linked to current and future well-being. Lerner attributes this emerging focus on strengths in part to increased collaboration among scholars, practitioners, and policy makers and a recent National Research Council (NRC) report[8] makes a similar observation. In simple terms captured by Pittman and colleagues, "problem-free is not fully prepared";[9] it is helpful to conceptualize successful development as larger than avoidance of problems. If we are going to intentionally try to create "pathways to successful youth development," we need to theorize success and its correlates.

As is reviewed in the NRC volume,[10] many theorists have proposed sets of assets,[11] including things such as possessing a sense of safety (emotional and physical), social connectedness, a desire to learn and be curious, and a sense of identity and meaning.[12] Many such lists have also been suggested by applied developmental scholars and practitioners.[13] The lists of important strengths and assets from theory, empirical studies, and practice have much common ground. The National Research Council, for instance, offers a summary derived from theory and empirical studies of programs, families, and other developmental contexts.[14]

How universal are the strengths and assets?

It is both theoretically and practically important to ask how universal or culturally specific these statements of important strengths and assets are. Anthropologists[15] and developmental psychologists[16] remind us that the meaning and manifestation of a particular strength—such as good health habits, or confidence in one's personal efficacy—vary by cultural context. Many authors have noted the need for more empirical work to help us understand how the particulars of strengths and assets or well-being vary by such factors as social identity, gender, place, developmental age, and historical time.

But it also appears, in this volume and elsewhere, that at some useful level of abstraction the various lists of strengths and assets converge. Said another way, thriving may look different according to age and cultural context, but it is a useful way to conceptualize successful youth development more universally.

Conditions linked to positive youth development

As theorists have worked to conceptualize development and its multiple, relational contexts, so too have scholars and practitioners tried to identify (1) the features that characterize productive person-context transactions and (2) positive configurations of such transactions across time and place. In the NRC volume, these are termed "the features of positive developmental settings" and in much of the applied, youth development literature they are described as the "supports and opportunities" that are linked to well-being.[17] As with the statements of strengths and assets, these supports and opportunities vary from one author to the next, but they also have much in common. The NRC volume suggests a set derived from theory and practice; Gambone[18] has summarized the differences and overlap among the taxonomies prominent in practice. Examples of items common to most lists are meaningful and supportive relationships with peers and adults, the opportunity to develop "hard" (academic, task-specific) and "soft" (relational, not job–specific) skills, and predictable limits that are developmentally and situationally appropriate. These supports and opportunities are linked with the well-being of youth, as shown in Figure 7.1.

This simple figure is meant to illustrate the reciprocal, transactional nature of the relationships between supports and opportuni-

Figure 7.1. The relationship among youth strengths and assets, supports and opportunities, and adult well-being

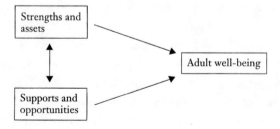

ties and youth strengths and assets. One does not cause the other. Rather, as Lerner, Taylor, and von Eye describe in the Editors' Notes of this volume, healthy development involves positive change in the relationship between a developing person and the surrounding environment. This is the same point made explicitly by Benson and colleagues in their conjoining of internal and external assets in the Search Institute framework.[19] Although it is possible to conceptualize strengths and assets as existing primarily in the person, theory suggests that they are meaningfully manifest only in the transaction between the person and environment.

Creating the conditions linked to positive youth development

Theory and empirical studies in applied developmental science have allowed us to agree on the markers of successful youth development and the conditions linked to it, but the field has done much less to help policy makers and practitioners understand how to intentionally intervene and enhance development. Systems theory describes interconnection of the elements in development, presenting the policy maker or practitioner with many places to start. For the sake of this chapter, the question is understood as, How can we improve the availability and quality of supports and opportunities for young people?

Creating intentional change

Work done by disparate scholars in various disciplines suggests that we have much to learn if we are to create the supports and opportunities young people need to thrive. Perhaps because the conscious focus on environmental influence is relatively recent, so too is the science around (1) societal change on behalf of youth or others (including individual, collective, organizational, and community change), (2) diffusion of social innovation, and (3) the role of evidence in policy making and practice. Prochaska and colleagues[20] have contributed theory and empirical work on changing individual behaviors such as smoking and overeating. Rogers[21] has for forty years described the diffusion of fairly technical innovation. Weiss[22] has analyzed the use of research in policy making. Skocpol[23] and Imig[24] have described the evolution of norm-oriented social movements, and various scholars have examined change in such applied settings as employment programs, community-based organizations, communities and neighborhoods, and schools.

Although these various scholars of change rarely cite each others' work, they all tend to work within a stage framework that suggests some period of contemplation of change (for instance, dissatisfaction with the status quo, or a vision that things can be better), initiation of change (most try to understand the factors that shape change and, if change involves adapting practices from another setting, how the practices are adapted to a local need), and institutionalization (determining what sustains change, or how one can take it to scale). This stage model is durable across several fields, although Mayer and Davidson[25] note that it is not clear that change is either so orderly or so self-conscious.

Points of agreement regarding intentional change

Reading across these literatures, we find that some lessons and common findings emerge. For example:

- Knowledge about new ways of achieving one's goal is a useful ingredient in planful change, but it is not enough to ensure that change occurs. Knowledge of the efficacy of immunization is not enough to persuade everyone to get one, and knowing about the importance of diet and exercise does not ensure a high-quality version of either.
- We like to learn about new practices or possibilities from people we know or trust. An enduring finding in the summaries of research on the diffusion of innovation by Rogers, this point was underscored in a recent scan of youth practitioners.[26] Pittman and Yohalem found that many practitioners and policy makers rely on individuals whom they personally know as a source of "what is known" about research in a given area.

- Change is unlikely to occur without dissatisfaction with the status quo and the knowledge, skills, and resources that support change. That is, change demands both *will* and *capacity* to change. (I return to these two constructs later, in discussing interventions primarily targeted on will or capacity.)
- The more complex and nuanced an issue is (as with almost all the questions concerning how to enhance human development), the greater the need for local ownership and iterative creation or adaptation of possible solutions.
- Interventions that fit existing practice, are seen as an improvement on the status quo, and are relatively simple are more likely to be adopted than interventions that lack these features.

In some sense, this accumulation of findings is promising because it has emerged from a number of disciplines and settings. The work is mostly descriptive, but it has considerable ecological validity in that most of the findings emerge from case studies of actual change efforts.

Recognizing the need for more definite, causal analysis regarding the effect of intervention, within the past twenty years many psychologists (particularly community psychologists) have designed and tested interventions meant to prevent various problems. An example is poor mental health.[27] Working within the National Institutes of Health (NIH) "intervention/prevention" cycle,[28] this usually involves successive, randomized, controlled trials testing new programs. Interventions are first implemented and assessed in a few places, with a constrained number and composition of participants, to determine if an intervention can make a difference. (This stage of the NIH cycle is known as the efficacy phase.) If shown to be efficacious, the intervention is tested more widely in effectiveness trials to assess its effects under broader conditions and populations.

Even at the effectiveness stage, the trials tend to be tightly controlled. Therefore, they offer only modest assurance that any observed effects created by the intervention can be achieved if it is tried at a scale that would make it common to most youth.

A research tradition that weds the methodological rigor of the NIH cycle with the external validity of descriptive, observational studies of change are the social experiments pioneered by the Manpower Demonstration Research Corporation (MDRC) in the welfare and employment field.[29] Now common in many policy areas,[30] this research and demonstration approach uses fully experimental designs to test policy and program intervention in multiple settings with a large number of participants.[31] This approach generates information that has proved to be credible and useful to policy makers regarding the effects of intervention.[32] However, the studies rarely yield information on how to create and institutionalize the intervention in diverse circumstances. The level of implementation is assessed to determine if the intervention got a fair test, but little work is done to explain variation in implementation.[33]

Descriptive and experimental work on change suggests a number of challenges for those interested in building a science of social change.[34] First, it could be useful to have a delineation of the strategies interventionists use to create change. Second, it is important to empirically link those strategies to improved supports and opportunities for youth. Third, we need an ongoing program of research that helps us understand how various strategies are linked to, and influenced by, supports and opportunities.

A framework for conceptualizing interventions meant to improve supports and opportunities

In the literature on planned individual, organizational, and systemic change, scholars emphasize will and capacity as the primary mediators of subsequent change. For change to occur, the intervention must influence the inclination or propensity to change (will), the ability to change (capacity), or both.

Figure 7.2 illustrates the relationships among intervention strategies, will and capacity, and supports and opportunities. As with development, the relationships depicted in the figure are seen as a

Figure 7.2. A framework linking intervention strategies to conditions for positive development

system that operates in a particular ecological niche. The primary pathway linking intervention strategy and supports and opportunities passes through the will and capacity to change. The existing levels and nature of will and capacity and supports and opportunities are likely to influence the choice of intervention strategy and the effectiveness of the strategy.

For example, assume that one is trying to influence the diversity and quality of meaningful relationships with adults in the lives of youth. A plausible intervention has to consider the will and capacity of the youth and proximal adults to create such a relationship, promising developmental settings (neighborhood, program, organization) susceptible to intervention, and the resources available for intervention. Having done so, those interested in change might conclude that the problem is primarily one of will and the best solution is use of public policy and various media to change incentives. Conversely, the problem may be understood as mostly one of capacity, with the need for education, training, or redistribution of income to permit different uses of time.

Admittedly, the formulation is abstract, in part because the phrase *intervention strategy* is underspecified. The next section of this chapter offers a start on a list of generic intervention strategies, analogous to the sets we now have of strengths and assets and supports and opportunities. Generated by considering the deeper structure of a number of attempts to influence youth development, the list is very much a work in progress that needs greater theoretical coherence. Strategies are listed as primarily intended to create the will or the capacity to change, but the distinction is blurred given the reciprocal nature of will and capacity.

Intervention strategies to enhance the will to change

To influence will, in a change effort five intervention strategies are commonly used (often in combination).

1. *Standards.* The standards approach to creating change includes output standards for programs and systems (such as educational standards for a state), design standards (perhaps for a professional preparation program), and equity standards (pushing for equality of opportunity, such as equity laws for school financing). The notion is that a consensus on goals, and benchmarks for those goals, will catalyze change.

2. *Availability of data.* This strategy includes providing data on problems and on areas addressed by standards, such as performance data; funding (equity) data; and data on the accessibility, affordability, and quality of resources such as programs and systems. For example, the Search Institute's work with communities nationwide[35] begins with providing data by way of an "assets inventory."

3. *Contingencies related to change.* This approach includes incentives and rewards for change (monetary reward, social recognition) and sanctions and punishments for lack of change (penalties, loss of funding, loss of access to goods and services). In general, this approach is about rewards and accountability for action.

4. *Social pressure.* This category includes such strategies as collective organizing, civil action, voting, and advocacy.

5. *Marketing and "messaging."* This group includes all forms of communication encouraging the need to change or information about opportunities for change (as with presentation of a new frame or persuasion campaign).

Although these five strategies are conceptually distinct, they are almost always used in combination. For example, social pressure and marketing strategies are often focused on the need for agreed-upon goals; in themselves, social pressure and marketing represent an attempt to change the contingencies regarding change.

Intervention strategies to enhance the capacity to change

Beyond will, the capacity to change is also required. Across interventions, these strategies fall into five approaches that are also commonly used in various combinations:

1. *Human capital creation.* These strategies emphasize education, training, or other ways to change human capital. Common examples are staff and leadership development.

2. *Redistribution strategies.* These are strategies meant to redistribute physical or economic capital for reasons of equity, efficiency, or some other social goal. For example, changing the earned income tax credit is an economic redistribution strategy in that it moves tax dollars from one set of citizens to others, conditioned on income and work.

3. *Investment strategies.* An investment strategy seeks to seed or foster subsequent capacity through an initial investment. Examples are a public subsidy for building a new school or other youth-serving facility, or a grant to allow scholars to form a network of scholars and practitioners.

4. *Social capital creation.* This category of intervention attempts to change the nature, density, and norms of human relationships. Examples are a structural change in a school that creates a smaller "community," reorganizing a program to get recruiters and direct-service staff together, creation of a new organization in a community, and mentoring.

5. *Efficiency strategies.* These are efforts to improve capacity by means of increased efficiency: service integration, integrated case management, creation of intermediaries to make a "sector" work better, and so on.

As with the intervention strategies focused on will, those emphasizing capacity are often used together. In addition, interventionists tend to focus on a particular developmental context (though not necessarily using that language). For example, interventions meant to directly affect individual youth are common (for example, expand a program, establish a new policy targeted on individual behavior). But so are interventions aimed at an organization, system, or community.

We can name these intervention approaches, but we know little about them in any way that could guide choices for policy and practice. Rather, we are left to experience "reform du jour," where a particular approach gains brief popularity, perhaps from poorly understood macro factors such as variation in national prosperity. After a period of time, the predominant paradigm changes, but we are left with little theoretical, empirical, or practical guidance regarding selection and implementation of intervention approaches.

Implications of this analysis for future work

Consensus regarding the utility of systems theory, and a focus on strengths and assets as well as supports and opportunities, is important for our future work in several ways. The strengths and assets give us a way to index and define success among young people. The supports and opportunities present a related way to describe positive conditions across developmental settings. System theory helps us realize the interconnections among these factors and implies the need to look to the configuration of the whole ecology.

This consensus has resulted from theory-driven, methodologically sophisticated work meant to understand the nature and trajectory of human development. Similarly, we have learned a lot from strong evaluation of the effects of intervention. Given the resources that public and private organizations spend on intervention meant to improve the well-being of young people, coupled with the countless "private" hours spent by adults and youth, it is discouraging that we know so little about how to create and sustain positive change at any scale.

This suggests the need for a body of work on a new set of questions that is just as strong as the best of our applied, developmental work on individual change. Because limits in human capital and financial resources demand priorities, we need to ask less about what young people need and focus much more on learning how to bring those conditions about.

In moving ahead, it may be useful to conceptualize the challenge as trying to enrich the supports and opportunities extant at some level in the lives of almost all youth. Because the literatures on intervention and change are so diverse and poorly connected, it would be useful to have syntheses of existing theory and empirical studies across fields; studies of the attempt to systematically intervene at one or more levels of the developmental system (individual, family, peers, organization, system, community); and work to theorize such intervention so that the literature feels less like individual evaluation and more like a coherent body of theory-testing, cumulative work.

Stating ten intervention strategies in this chapter is a start down this road, because the (tentative) claim is that these ten strategies are a step toward a taxonomy of interventions. But we now need to understand how the system linking intervention with support and opportunity operates with different people, places, and times. Particular studies are likely to focus on specific units of analysis (such as the individual, organization, or system), but the current developmental theory exemplified by this volume forces our attention on the relationships among them. Over time, such a research agenda has a chance to help us understand what it takes for all youth to experience the successful development enjoyed now by only some of them.

Notes

1. Harlow, H. F., and Suomi, S. J. (1970). The nature of love simplified. *American Psychologist, 25,* 161–168; Dennis, W. (1941). Infant development under conditions of restricted practice and of minimum social stimulation. *Genetic Psychology Monographs, 23,* part 1, 142–191.

2. Hunt, J. McV. (1961). *Intelligence and experience.* New York: Ronald Press.

3. Piaget, J. (1954). *The construction of reality in the child.* New York: Basic Books.

4. Bronfenbrenner, U. (1979). *The ecology of human development: Experiments by nature and design.* Cambridge, MA: Harvard University Press.

5. Lerner, R. M. (2002). *Concepts and theories of human development* (3rd ed., p. 187). Mahwah, NJ: Erlbaum; Spencer, M. B. (1995). Old issues and new theorizing about African American youth: A phenomenological variant of the ecological systems theory. In R. L. Taylor (ed.), *Black youth: Perspectives on their status in the United States.* New York: Praeger.

6. Lerner (2002).

7. Lerner, R. M. (1984). *On the nature of human plasticity.* New York: Cambridge University Press; Bronfenbrenner, U., and Morris, P. (1998). The ecology of developmental process. In W. Damon and R. Lerner (eds.), *Handbook of child psychology* (5th ed.). New York: Wiley.

8. National Research Council and Institute of Medicine. (2002). In J. Eccles and J. A. Gootman (Eds.), *Community programs to promote youth development.* Washington, D.C.: National Academy Press.

9. Pittman, K. J., and Irby, M. (1996). *Preventing problems or promoting development: Competing priorities or inseparable goals?* Takoma Park, MD: International Youth Foundation.

10. National Research Council and Institute of Medicine (2002).

11. Erikson, E. (1963). *Childhood and society.* New York: Norton; Harter, S. (1998). The development of self-representations. In W. Damon and N. Eisenberg (Eds.), *Handbook of child psychology: Social, emotional, and personality development* (5th ed.). New York: Wiley; Bandura, A. (1994). *Self-efficacy: The exercise of control.* New York: Freeman; Lerner, R. M., Fisher, C. B., and Weinberg, R. A. (2000). Toward a science for and of the people: Promoting civil society through the application of developmental science. *Child Development, 71,* 11–20.

12. National Research Council and Institute of Medicine (2002).

13. Benson, P. L. (1997). *All kids are our kids: What communities must do to raise caring and responsible children and adolescents.* San Francisco: Jossey-Bass; Pittman, K. J., Ferber, T., and Irby, M. (2000). Unfinished business: Further reflections on a decade of promoting youth development. Takoma Park, MD: International Youth Foundation; Connell, J. P., Gambone, M. A., and Smith, T. (2000). Youth development in community settings. In Public/Private Ventures (Ed.), *Youth development: Issues, challenges and directions.* Philadelphia: Public/Private Ventures; Carnegie Corporation of New York. (1992). *A matter of time: Risk and opportunity in the nonschool hours.* (Task Force on Youth Development and Community Programs and Carnegie Council on Adolescent Development.) New York: Carnegie Corporation.

14. National Research Council and Institute of Medicine (2002).

15. Weisner, T. S. (1996). Why ethnography should be the most important method in the study of human development. In R. Jessor, A. Colby, and R. Shweder (Eds.), *Ethnography and human development: Context and meaning in social inquiry.* Chicago: University of Chicago Press; Weisner, T. S. (2001). Anthropological aspects of childhood. In *International encyclopedia of the social sciences, vol. 3.* Oxford: Elsevier Science; Shweder, R. A., Goodnow, J., Hatano, G., LeVine, R. A., Markus, H., and Miller, P. (1998). The cultural psychology of development: One mind many mentalities. In W. Damon (Series Ed.) & R. M. Lerner (Vol. Ed.), *Handbook of child psychology: Vol. 1. Theoretical models of human development* (5th ed., pp. 865–937). New York: Wiley.

16. See Chapter Four of this volume. See also Garcia-Coll, C. T., and Magnuson, K. (2000). Cultural differences as sources of developmental vulnerabilities and resources: A view from developmental research. In S. J. Meisels and J. P. Shonkoff (Eds.), *Handbook of early childhood intervention*. Cambridge: Cambridge University Press.

17. Pittman, Ferber, & Irby (2000); Connell, Gambone, & Smith (2000).

18. Gambone, M. A. (in press). Community action and youth development: What can be done and how can we measure progress?" In K. Fulbright-Anderson and P. Auspos (Eds.), *Community change: Theories, practice, and evidence*. Washington, D.C.: Aspen Institute.

19. Scales, P. C., and Leffert, N. (1999). *Developmental assets: A synthesis of scientific research on adolescent development*. Minneapolis: Search Institute; and Chapter Six of this volume.

20. Prochaska, J. O. (1999). How do people change, and how can we change to help many more people? In M. A. Hubble and L. Barry (Eds.), *The heart and soul of change: What works in therapy*. Washington, D.C.: American Psychological Association.

21. Rogers, E. V. (1995). *Diffusion of innovations* (4th ed.). New York: Free Press.

22. Weiss, C. H. (1997). *Using social research in public policy making*. Lexington, MA: Lexington/Health Books.

23. Skocpol, T., et al. (1999). How Americans become civic. In T. Skocpol and M. P. Fiorina (Eds.), *Civic engagement in American democracy*. Washington, D.C.: Brookings Institution Press, and New York: Russell Sage Foundation.

24. Imig, D. (2001). Who speaks for America's children?: The role of child advocates in public policy. In C. DeVita and R. Mosher-Williams (Eds.), *Mobilizing parents and communities for children*. Washington, D.C.: Urban Institute Press.

25. Mayer, J. P., and Davidson, W. S., II. (2000). Dissemination of innovation as social change. In J. Rappaport and E. Seidman (Eds.), *Handbook of community psychology*. New York: Kluwer Academic/Plenum.

26. Yohalem, N., and Pittman, K. (in press). *Identifying and mapping key ideas in the youth field*. (Working paper.) New York: William T. Grant Foundation.

27. Imig (2001).

28. National Institute of Mental Health. (1993). *The Prevention of Mental Disorders: A National Research Agenda*. Rockville, MD: National Institute of Mental Health.

29. Gueron, J. M. (2002). The politics of random assignment: Implementing studies and affecting policy. In F. Mosteller and R. Boruch (Eds.), *Evidence matters: Randomized trials in education research*. Washington, D.C.: Brookings Institution.

30. Boruch, R. F. (1997). *Randomized experiments for planning and evaluation*. Thousand Oaks, CA: Sage.

31. National Institute of Mental Health (1993).

32. Baum, E. B. (1991). When the witch doctors agree: The Family Support Act and social science research. *Journal of Policy Analysis and Management*, *10*(4), 603–615; Szanton, P. L. (1991). The remarkable "Quango": Knowledge, politics, and welfare reform. *Journal of Policy Analysis and Management*, *10*(4), 590–602.

33. Doolittle, F., and Sherwood, K. E. (in press). What's behind the impacts: Doing implementation research in the context of program impact studies. In T. Corbett and M. C. Lennon (Eds.), *Implementation analysis: An evaluation approach whose time has come.* Washington, D.C.: Urban Institute Press.

34. Scales & Leffert (1999).

35. Benson, P. L., Leffert, N., Scales, P. C., and Blyth, D. A. (1998). Beyond the village rhetoric: Creating health communities for children and adolescents. *Applied Developmental Science, 2*(3), 138–159.

ROBERT C. GRANGER *is senior vice president of the William T. Grant Foundation, in New York City.*

Index

Achievement: and assets, 133, 136; pressure for, 110–111, 112

Adams, G. R., 89

Adolescents: engagement of, 140; normal behavior of, 113; number of assets of, 131–132; problem-free *versus* prepared, 133–134; and societal inconsistency, 91–92; variation in assets of, 131; vocabulary describing development of, 11–12

Adolescents, affluent: achievement pressure of, 110–111, 112; characteristics of parents of, 115; distress of, 112–115, 115–116; and drug use, 103–104, 106–107, 108–109, 110, 114, 116; lack of supervision of, 116; maladaption of, 110–113; and parent closeness, 103, 111–112, 116–117; peer ratings of, 107; *versus* poor adolescents, 103, 106–107; research on, 106–113; supports for, 113; well-being of, 106

Adolescents, poor: *versus* affluent adolescents, 103, 106–107; assets of, 36; and drug use, 103–104; and gender identity, 81; peer ratings of, 105–106; research on, 105–106

Adults: engagement of, 140, 141; generative, 26

Adverse outcomes, 78

African American community-based organization youth: *versus* African American gang members, 36–38; assets of, 36–37, 44, 47, 50–51, 68–69; research on, 38–49, 59–68

African American gang members: *versus* African American youth in community-based organizations, 36–38; assets of, 36–37, 44, 47, 50–51, 68–69; characteristics of positive development in, 37–38; and deficit view of development,

50; improved quality of life for, 69; research on, 38–49, 59–68

African American youth: conceptual flaws about, 74; coping responses of, 77–78; effects of socialization of, 82; expectations of, 88, 89; and father absence, 80–81; feedback to, 88–89, 90; gender identity of, 80–85; identity development of, 75; masculinity of, 81, 83; obesity of, 84–85; outcomes of, 78; and relationship between racial identity and academic achievement, 90–91; risk factors for, 76–77; school experiences of, 86–91; self-views of, 78; and spiritual development, 91–94; stereotypes of, 75, 82–83; stressors of, 77; supports of, 77, 82, 83; teacher evaluations of, 88; teachers' perceptions of, 87–88; teachers' predictions of success for, 89

Alcohol use, 114

Ancestors, protohominid, 18–19

Anderson, P. M., 5, 6, 11, 35, 57

Anxiety rates, 106

Applied developmental science, 15, 17–18

Asset-based community development, 124

Asset-building community, 124, 138–142

Assets: and achievement, 133, 136; of African American gang members *versus* community-based organization youth, 36–37, 44, 47, 50–51, 68–69; categories of, 127–129; conditions for manifestation of, 152–153; consensus on, 151–152, 160; cumulative nature of, 132, 133–134; family as, 134–135; impact on intervention research, 160; infusion with development,

Back Issue/Subscription Order Form

Copy or detach and send to:

Jossey-Bass, A Wiley Company, 989 Market Street, San Francisco CA 94103-1741

Call or fax toll-free: Phone 888-378-2537; Fax 888-481-2665

Back Issues: Please send me the following issues at $28 each
(Important: please include issue ISBN)

_____

_____

$ _____   Total for single issues

$ _____   SHIPPING CHARGES: SURFACE   Domestic   Canadian

		Domestic	Canadian
	First Item	$5.00	$6.00
	Each Add'l Item	$3.00	$1.50

Please call for next day, second day, or international shipping rates.

Subscriptions   Please ❑ start ❑ renew my subscription to *New Directions for Youth Development* at the following rate:

U.S.	❑ Individual $75	❑ Institutional $149
Canada	❑ Individual $75	❑ Institutional $189
All Others	❑ Individual $99	❑ Institutional $223
Online Subscription		❑ Institutional $149

**For more information about online subscriptions visit
www.interscience.wiley.com**

-- _____   Are you eligible for our **Student Subscription Rate**? Attach a copy of your current Student Identification Card and deduct 20% from the regular subscription rate.

$ _____   Total single issues and subscriptions (Add appropriate sales tax for your state for single issue orders. No sales tax for U.S. subscriptions. Canadian residents, add GST for subscriptions and single issues.)

❑ Payment enclosed (U.S. check or money order only)

❑ VISA ❑ MC ❑ AmEx ❑ Discover Card # _____ Exp. Date _____

Your credit card payment will be charged to John Wiley & Sons.

Signature _____ Day Phone _____

❑ Bill Me (U.S. institutional orders only. Purchase order required.)

Purchase order # _____

Federal Tax ID13559302   **GST 89102 8052**

Name _____

Address _____

_____

Phone _____ E-mail _____

PROMOTION CODE ND3

Printed in the United States
121488LV00005B/2/A